The Art of Eroticism

Published in the United States of America.
First edition.

The Art of Eroticism
HPJ Writeeasy Publishing
ISBN (Trade pbk.)
ISBN # 978-1-7330502-5-8
Layout and Design: Dasan Ahanu
Cover Photo: Tyrone Combs
Cover Design: Dasan Ahanu

HPJ Writeeasy Publishing
Durham, NC

To the man or woman that is reading this book: Love yourself. Love each other. Be safe. Be selective. Protect your mind and body at all times, and don't share any level of intimacy with someone who doesn't respect you as much as you do!

Whether you are reading this because you love erotica, because you want some ideas, or because you are just trying to unwind with some entertainment from a stressful day, I hope you enjoy this collection of work!

Stay Sexy!

-Debrita "Wild Perfection" Channelle

Table of Contents

Let Them See

Slowly,
Wrap your lips around my finger and taste excellence,
Never mind the people who paid $12.50 to enjoy a 3D movie,
Let them see.
Let them see what it's like to be taken at any moment,
To be craved more than over-buttered popcorn.
I've always had a thing for being seen.
I guess you can call me an exhibitionist,
And I don't think many people realize that they
Are voyeurs until they are given
The opportunity to watch
"I don't give a fuck" fucking in person so,
Push me back...
Let me rest my head on the lap of the woman next to me,
while you devour your anticipation,
Let her see your thick tongue,
with ninja like precision,
Let people be irate.
Not that they are missing the movie
or because of our inability to wait,
but let them rowel themselves up with anger,
because they aren't cuming
nearly as many times as you're making me.
Spread me like a blueprint.
Bring my knee to my forehead,
And eat the ass that you can sometimes be,
Show them what beautifully nasty looks like.
Pull down the cup holders to keep me from running,
bend me over my seat and let me see.
Eyes, illuminated...
Fuck Netflix and chill,
This will be Regal Cinemas and thrill

and we won't even be able to make it past the previews,
before you roll your own credits,
for the production we put on.
This scene will be beyond R or NC-17,
Our freak has not yet been rated,
This, will be for mature
And non-judgmental audiences only,
So, grab my waist...
pull me back on to Black Snake,
Start slow like Forest Gump with leg brace,
Then, speed up like Vin Diesel on a clutch,
This will be fast and furious,
The way you pull my hair should resemble a Tokyo drift,
As intense as Al Pacino,
Then Pound me violently,
Like Quentin Tarantino directed this scene himself,
with orgasms blasting like bullets,
Like this is Django,
And Broomhilda has been waiting for you in my confides
of my G-spot,
Show me...
Show them what we're here for...
What real life Oscar Worthy love-making scenes look like,
when you're as disciplined in each other as we...
So I'm going to dip my finger in my panties
and place it on your lips...
And, when you taste it... let them see...

Steve's Bakery

It was a Superbowl Sunday evening that was a lot warmer than it should have been. Everyone was either at home or at a bar, enjoying what was an American Holiday. I peeped through the glass window of his bakery. He usually had plenty of customers and was busy but it was almost closing time and traffic was slow. When I walked in he was handing over a boxed cake to a customer at the register.

"Thanks Steve!" the customer said. "I really appreciate you doing this late notice. If I went to this party without this cake, my sister would kill me." She chuckled and turned to leave.

"No problem Tara. And tell your sister I said to bring her busy ass by here sometimes to see me."

"I know! She got big and forgot about us little people, right?"

"She sure did!" Steve said laughing. "Alright, take care!"

"See you later!" the customer said heading for the door.

I held it open for her so she wouldn't risk dropping the cake.

"Holding doors for people? You must be in a good mood." He said grinning.

"You calling me a bitch?" I asked playfully.

"Not at all. I'm just saying that you rarely hold the door for people."

"I'm working on that Southern Hospitality thing." I said to him leaning on the front door. "Are you closing?"

"Yea, I might as well. Go ahead and lock the door and turn that sign over for me." He said, taking the pastries out of the display cases to take to the back.

I did what I was told then took my jacket off and sat it on the table.

He appeared from the back with one of the trays in his hand. "You planning to help me clean up?"
"Actually I'm planning on making a mess. But you can take those trays to the back first." I said playing with my keys.
He walked to the back, acting like he didn't know what I was saying. "I don't know what kind of mess you plan on making but let me clean some of this stuff up first." He yelled. I sighed. He was going to make me be more obvious. I walked over the counter and sat on it, next to the register.
"How long is it going to take you to put everything away?" I yelled to him.
"Usually forty minutes but I still have to sweep and mop!" That was too long for me. He appeared again, going for the tray of cupcakes in the display. I hit the bell that was on his countertop a good five times. He sat the tray of cupcakes on the other side of the counter and stood beside me.
"Can I help you?" he asked, wiping his hands on his apron.
"Yes, I would like one of those chocolate cupcakes you have on the tray please."
He shook his head and reached over to hand me a Double chocolate cupcake. I could smell its sweetness from the tray. My mouth was already watering.
"Thank you." I said, before biting into its sugariness. "This is delicious."
"It is. Can I get you anything else?" Steve seemed adamant about finishing the cleaning. He probably wanted to get home to catch the rest of the game. But I was hoping to make a touchdown of my own. We heard a knock on the door. I looked back.
"We're closed!" Steve yelled, pointing to the 'Closed' sign. The man shook his head and walked away disappointed. The way he shook his head told me that he really wanted something sweet that night. We both were craving something.

Steve started to walk away from me, but I grabbed his arm.
"What is it?" He asked. I didn't care about his annoyance with me. I just wanted him to entertain my wants for a moment.
"Come here." I said, pulling him between my legs. I stuck my finger in the icing from the cupcake and told him to taste it. He wrapped his juicy lips around my finger and sucked the icing off.
"How does it taste?" I asked.
"Like you." He responded leaning in to kiss me. I could taste the chocolate on his tongue. I wrapped my legs around him.
"Baby, I really have to clean up so we can get out of here." He said.
"Why do we need to leave?" I asked kissing his cheeks.
"So we can finish this at home." He said, squeezing my ass through my leggings. He wanted me... Bad.
"Why can't we do it here?" I asked, touching my nose to his. I didn't want him to think too hard about it, so I followed my suggestion with a longer kiss. He reached to put his hands under my shirt, accidentally getting icing on himself from the cupcake I was still holding.
"Let me get that." I said, pulling his forearm up to my lips and licking the icing off hungrily. I watched him bite his bottom lip while he stared at my tongue. I put the cupcake down and pulled him in close to go for his neck. Then reached around him to untie his apron and pull it off.
"The lights are still on. People can see us."
"So? Let them see." I said grinning. The lights in the bakery at night were dim anyway, and the streets were almost empty. If there was anyone walking past, I wanted them to see the fun I was having. The thought of them looking excited me. I kicked my shoes off and lifted my ass in the air so he could pull my leggings and panties off. He pulled my low cut shirt down, pulling my breasts out of my bra with ease. He grabbed a container of buttercream frosting off the back counter, dipped his

fingers in it and wrote his name across my chest, with the "S" starting over my right nipple and "e" ending on the other. I cupped the back of his head in my hand as I felt his salivating tongue lick across the letters, carefully. I began moaning. He loved my twins so much that he could lick them forever if I allowed him. He licked and caressed and put the perfect amount of pressure on them for sensitivity. I could've cum from that alone but my womb cried out for him. I unbuttoned his pants and put my hands inside his boxers so I could slide them off at once. He pulled my ass closer to the edge of the counter for the perfect entrance angle. I felt his dick bump my thigh and my pussy throbbed with excitement. He kissed me and then held my bottom lip between his teeth. As he entered me he bit my lip harder. For every inch he pushed into me, he put more pressure into his bite. That made me wetter. Once he was all the way inside, he let go of my lip and pressed his cheek against mine, facing the store front.

"Is this what you wanted?" He said, stroking slowly.

I moaned in response "Mmm hmmm."

The wetness my insides produced made the glide easy. I wrapped both of my hands around his neck, bringing him even closer. I could feel my walls tightening. "Lay back" he instructed me. And I did… with my back against the cold counter. I ended up with my head hanging off the edge, and as soon as I looked toward the windows, I could see 5 figures there. I sat up quickly and turned around, making sure my eyes weren't deceiving me. There were indeed 5 people standing in front, watching us through the windows- One couple and three others. Steve began sucking on my earlobe.

"You wanted them to see, right?" he asked. I smirked, and then turned back around to face him. I did want them to see. I just didn't know it would happen so quickly.

"How long have they been there?" I asked him. He responded by tonguing me down intensely and pushing me back against the countertop. I almost feel like he wanted them to watch us more than I did. With my head dangling upside down again, I looked at the five figures watching us. Steve opened my legs wide and started thrusting again, deeper.

"Shit!" I said, feeling him in my stomach. I closed my eyes, concentrating on trying to relax my pussy. I clenched my teeth and moaned every time he hit my cervix. But then he went harder, forcing me to moan louder. I put my hands on his waist to keep him from going too deep.

"Move your hands." He commanded.

"It's too deep!" I whined to him, gasping for air.

"Move your hands!" He repeated. I stopped pushing his torso back and grabbed anything that could pull me up from his thick dick. I pushed the register, which pushed the tray of cupcakes onto the floor. Steve had my legs locked with his arms. By this time, I was screaming. I knew the people outside the Bakery could hear me but there was no way I could keep those noises suppressed. I felt my orgasm creeping toward the surface every time he slid his dick back. He was literally pulling it out of me. I grabbed onto his arms, squeezing them and bracing myself for the intensity.

With my mouth open, I moaned "Shit, Steven!" My body got stiff. I held my breath and felt myself release. My arms shook from the tight grip I had on him. I held him that way until I felt my walls relax again. He pulled out of me, grinning like he just received an award for his performance. My body fell limp and I relaxed myself, laying back and looking at the people outside of the window again. I watched the couple, with the man standing behind the girl and his hands around her waist, whispering something in her ear. Probably something he was inspired to do to her when they left. I couldn't really make out their faces but I imagined he was telling her he was going to fuck her on the hood of his car in the parking lot. Something as adventurous as what they had just witnessed. That thought made me smile.

I sat up to look at Steven who was pulling his pants up. He was energized, doing everything with extra pep. "Are you going to help me clean?" He asked with his hands on my thighs.
"I guess I should since I made a mess on your counter."
"And the floor." He said referring to the cupcakes I'd knocked over. We laughed. "I'll get the supplies" He said heading to the back. I looked at the window to find that our audience had left. I wanted to be seen and that's exactly what I got. I had to chuckle to myself. I guess next time I should be more prepared for what I ask for.

Yes, Ma'am

I wiped my leather platform high heeled boots on the mat outside. It was freezing and raining, the perfect weather for high libidos. I put the 2 grocery bags I was carrying on the counter and put my coat on the back of the kitchen chair. That coat was essential in keeping my thigh high pantyhose and garter snaps concealed at the grocery store, along with hiding the fact that I wasn't wearing any panties. My boots showed a little knee but not enough to tip anyone off. The looks I got however were unforgettable. Those boots always brought attention, in public and at home. Letting my hair back down, I took a look in the hallways mirror, straightened my corset and walked into the back bathroom. "Marcus" I called out.

"Yes ma'am." I heard from behind the shower curtain. I pulled the curtains back, looking at this fine specimen standing exactly where I left him... With his hands tied to the showerhead.

"My arms are killing me." He whined, trying to look back at me over his shoulder.

"Are you complaining?" I snapped back.

"No ma'am." He replied.

"Just for that you're going to stand here and take a cold shower while I put up the groceries." I turned the shower on, as cold as it could get and closed the curtain again.

"Aaahhhhh!" I heard him yell, as I laughed silently under my breath and walked back to the kitchen. As I set the food out that was to be cooked, I could still hear him shouting and trying to get through the feeling of the freezing water on his body. That part was simply for my entertainment.

After putting everything away, I walked back into the shower to turn it off.

"Are you done complaining?" I asked.
"Yes ma'am." He replied shivering.
"Awww... you're shaking. Let me get you out." I untied his hands and made him step out as I wiped him from head to toe, moving the towel slowly from limb to limb.
"Are you cold?" I asked, after making sure he was dry.
"Yes."
"Yes what?"
"Yes ma'am."
"If you forget again, you are getting punished. Do you understand?"
"Yes... Ma'am." He responded with his hands covering his genitals.
"Are you touching yourself?"
"No ma'am." I looked him in the face, pretending I was trying to see if he was lying. I knew he wasn't but it didn't matter because all I needed was an excuse to torture him. I took the bondage tape off the sink and tied his hands behind his back.
"This is to make sure you don't touch yourself. Do you understand?"
"Yes ma'am." He said, shaking his head.
"Have you had enough?"
"No ma'am." His voice vibrated from the chills running through his body. It had not yet recovered from the cold shower.
"Are you cold down there?" I asked smirking.
"Yes ma'am."
I placed my hands on him, holding him with both hands at first. "Does that feel better??"
"Yes Ma'am." He said, relaxing. I left to grab warming massage oil from the bedroom and put a little on my hand. I went back into the bathroom and began groping him... Stroking his dick with my hands, making sure it was well coated. I looked into his eyes, purposely making things more pleasurable for him. I licked his shoulder and his neck. I should feel his temperature rising.
"What's the third rule Marcus?" I asked, continuing to stroke him.

"Don't cum without your permission." He said, looking away from me. That meant things were really starting to feel good to him.
"Look at me." I commanded. He looked down at me, clenching his jaw, trying not to show that he was enjoying the feeling.
"If you are about to cum, you tell me. Do you understand?"
"Yes ma'am." I pushed him against the sink, knowing he would need support since his legs were getting weaker. I moved my hand faster, wanting to pull a nut out of him. He moaned, closing his eyes and trying not to cum.
"Kiss me..." I whispered to him, allowing him to take control of his tongue in my mouth. He kissed me hard, while moaning. I moaned back. I loved pleasuring him. I loved the sound of his voice in ecstasy. His leg began to tremble.
"I'm about to cum." He exclaimed, pulling his face away from me. I bit his neck, pushing him closer to his nut, and right before the release point, I completely stopped everything. He moaned in agony, and I grinned knowing how it hurt that I wouldn't let him do it. I put my hands on both sides of him on the sink and kissed his chest. He shook his head, having no clue what I was going to do next... I pulled him into the bedroom by his dick, carefully, making sure not to hurt that beautiful monster. I sat him in the chair and got on my knees. I rubbed my face against his hardness, humming at the feel of him. Then I stuck my tongue out and licked him from the base to the tip. He sucked in air through his teeth and bit his lip. I licked him again, this time from his cum containers to his top. He moaned and I looked at him with a sinister grin. I let his tip massage my tongue before I sucked it like a Popsicle. The liquid he was producing from his tip was delicious. I grabbed his thighs and went to work, slurping and slobbering and making a mess in my desk chair. His legs began trembling again and a look of pain shot across his face which meant I was getting close. He pushed away from me but my mouth stayed on him.

"I'm about to come." He grunted. Again, I waited until the last possible moment before I took my mouth off of him. "Ahhhh!" He yelled, this time stomping his foot on the ground. Not being able to cum pained him. It was entertaining to see him so frustrated.

I still wasn't done with him yet... I pulled him by his dick again into the kitchen and sat him in a chair at the kitchen table, pushing him as close to it as I could comfortably get him. I sat on the table in front of him and placed my heels on the arms of the chair.

"Watch me. And don't put your mouth anywhere unless I say so. Do you understand?"

"Yes ma'am." He replied, looking like a sick puppy. I laid back and pushed myself to the edge of the table, right in front of his face. I was already ridiculously wet from pleasing him. Wetting 2 fingers with my juices, I began playing with my clitoris, moaning and squirming from the slippery friction. I slid my clit between two fingers and pressed them together. It almost felt like two lips sucking it but I was missing the warmth of a mouth. Marcus licked his lips like he was dehydrated and my pussy was the fountain of nourishment. I put my finger inside myself and then pointed it towards his mouth. He looked at me, wanting a command. I put the wet finger on his lips and made a circle around them.

"Mm, Mm, Mm." He said licking his lips. I put my finger back inside, took it out again and started making circles around my clit. This always made me cum.

"Kiss my thighs." I instructed him. He began kissing and licking my inner thighs slowly like they both had pussies on them. My orgasm started creeping up on me. The moans got shorter and stronger.

"I'm about to cum." I heard him say softly, moaning while he spoke.

I looked down at him, with his hands still behind his back. I had no clue he could cum without any stimulation to his dick. I was intrigued, so this time I didn't stop him.

"You can cum now." I said. I wanted to see him release it this way. I sat up and leaned on my arm, still making circles with my other hand and moaning. The way he bit my thigh let me know that nut was about to be something serious. That sent my body into an unexpected orgasm and I came so hard on that kitchen table. Marcus released soon after, clinching his teeth and making every vowel sound he could manage. I watched that warm clear liquid shoot all over his stomach and thigh. He shook as if electricity had struck his body, sucking in air like it hurt. It was the most erotic thing I had ever seen. When the excitement had lessened, he put his head down, panting hard. I sat there waiting for him to look at me. I wasn't sure if he was embarrassed or just exhausted. I put my hand under his chin and lifted his head up.

"Have you ever done that before?"

"No. Never." He said, almost in disbelief that he did that himself. I slid off the table and leaned over the chair to kiss him.

"That was so sexy, baby." I said, stroking the chin of his goatee. He grinned and shook his head. I had so many new experiences with him, I had lost count. But hands-free cumming had to be at the top of my favorite moments. "Thank you for giving that to me."

"Every time." He responded. I kissed him again and began to unravel the tape on his hands.

"After I clean you, you're going to go into the kitchen and make me something to eat. Understood?"

"Yes." He said smiling wide.

"Yes what?"

"Yes Ma'am."

Thor's Hammer

I thought you were joking...
When you told me your dick would
Hit me like Thor's hammer,
Or that your hands would smack
My ass until the red bottom was not my
Christian Louboutins....
I'm pretty sure you just fucked my life up.
My insides feel like jello,
From how much you banana'ed my pudding.
I'm trying to tell my uterus I'm sorry,
But she can't hear beyond the constant ringing
Of my ovaries...
I'm trying to do some kegels but you
Busted my shit completely open
And how I'm leaking like broken water slides.
I love you...
No I don't...
I didn't just say that...
You've fucked me into hallucinations,
And last night I felt,
The Rumble of Muhammad Ali,
In my stomach,
How you, pounded your power into me.
I'm looking at you right now as you sleep,
And I'm fighting my sanity.
Because Orgasms went off like bombs,
And each time my crazy level went up a tier,
And you reminded me there were levels,
And this was level 1 right here...
Out of 7 layers,
You asked me whose cake this was...
And we let ass smack against thigh so hard that
Wind could blow fire out,

And I thought "These must be trick candles
Cuz this shit is still flames"
Your hands gripping shoulders,
So I can't stop drop or roll,
Smokey the bear would be so disappointed.
Because i was producing so much water,
But it only seemed to make your fire grow.

Before you went to sleep...
I told you I thought your lashings brought on blood early...
And you said
"Periods...
Don't stop shit but a sentence...
You will still catch this dick like a flu,
So take some pain reliever,
Probiotics, and a nap before round 2"
And since, I know you're not joking,
I'm scared to move
Because I don't want to wake you up.
Because I don't want to end up...
Being that girl that's stalking all your social media pages,
Whenever i don't hear from you.
And your shit is way too good for you to be giving it to anybody else,
I will stab you, I am your girlfriend now!
And it's taking all the energy in me
Not to count your eyelashes,
But sex is my love language,
And you can speak it properly or in Ebonics,
You conjugated my body
With a mouth so perfect,
I can only think about you in future tense.
You will wake up and fuck these thoughts out of my head,
With the camera on,
So I can see if i captured the out of body phenomenon,
I keep having at your expense,
Our souls mixing like this
Is paranormal,

I know I'm not making sense,
But it doesn't make sense how good your dick is!
It and I seem to go on and on with no
Intention of clarity.
I think I will pray right now,
For our future.
Because right now I need you in it.
But I'll make sure to whisper
Because I don't want to wake you up
And honestly, I don't know if I'm really ready for what I'm asking for.

Yes, Daddy

I checked my watch. It was 10:30pm. She was late. I sighed and took a gulp from the bottle of red wine I had in my hand. I hated waiting. I was sitting on the edge of our bed, had the candles lit, a bottle in my hand that I had almost finished, and I put on a suit for her that I'd just purchased. She couldn't resist me in a suit. She got me with that shit she pulled that last time. I got her ass this time. I just needed her to walk through that door.

Just as I was thinking this night wasn't going to happen, I heard the door open. I waited quietly to hear her voice.

"Marcus, baby?" I heard her yell out. I was quiet. I heard her heels click across the kitchen floor. She was probably sitting her bags down from work. "Marcus!?" She called out again. I didn't respond. I was kind of pissed that I had been waiting on her for an hour. I waited a while until I heard the bedroom door knob twist. She opened the door as it squeaked slightly. I looked up at her. She grinned at me. I didn't return the expression.

"Hey baby, I-"

"-You're late." I said, interrupting her and looking at my watch.

"I am." She responded, looking at me like I was a piece of pie. "Baby, that suit-"

"-Why are you late?" I asked her, interrupting her again. My face was serious. She was startled.

"I got caught up with work."

"Put your coat down and come over here." It took all the strength in me not to fold, looking at her in that pencil skirt, fitting around the curve of her ass just right. But held my composure. She stood in front of me, leaning against the dresser. I took another gulp from my bottle. There was no use in sharing. It was almost gone. That was her fault for being late.

"I don't like waiting." I said. "It's been an hour." She was starting to catch where I was going. I watched as a smirk started to form across her face. "I'm sorry, is something funny?"

"No."

"No, what?" I asked. She paused before coming up with the proper response. "No, daddy."

"You're really fucking up my night." I said, sighing. I thought for a moment. "What should I do with you?"

"Whatever you think I deserve." She said, pouting her lips at me. .

"Wrong answer. Take your shirt off." I commanded, laying back on the bed to watch her. She stared at me while she did it, still trying to control the situation with her eyes. Any other time it would have worked, but not tonight. After she threw her shirt to the side, I commanded she take off her shoes and her skirt. I wanted her to leave her pantyhose on, since she wasn't wearing panties. "Get on your knees" I told her. She dropped to the floor and looked up at me as I stood over her. I pulled her hair back from her face and put it behind her ears. I then unzipped my pants, took my third arm out and put it in her face. She stuck her tongue out immediately. "Nuh uh... You don't do shit unless I tell you."

"Yes, daddy." She said, licking her lips. She wanted so bad to taste me. I was hard, anticipating contact with the back of her throat. I tilted her head back and rubbed the tip across her lips and smacked it across her cheek. She closed her eyes and sighed, lusting for its smoothness.

"Open your mouth." I told her, as she opened wide for me. I put it in slowly, feeling the warmth. She wrapped her lips around me tight. I held her hair in my hands, moving her head back and forth on me. Going a little deeper each time. Then I pushed myself in as far as I

could go, making her gag. I pulled her head back just before she choked. She looked up at me, eyes watery.
"I'm going to ask you again. What should I do with you?"
"Anything you want, Daddy." She said.
"Wrong answer." I said, and immediately started fucking her mouth again. I forcefully pushed it deeper, making her gag over and over. I then pulled her head back. "I'm going to ask you one more time. What should I do with you?"
"Punish me, daddy." She said, tears streaming from her eyes and panting heavily.
"Good girl." I said, then pulled her up from the floor.
"Turn around" I said, making her face the dresser to see herself in the mirror. Her mascara had started running. I stood behind her and put my hands on the outside of her thighs and felt my way up to her backside. "You're going to do as I say. If you don't, there will be consequences. Do you understand?"
"Yes, daddy."
I took my tie off and blindfolded her with it, making it as tight as I could get it without hurting her. "Can you see?" I asked.
"No, daddy."
"Good." I stepped away from her in order to give her the proper instructions. "Turn around, again." She turned around to face the bed. "Crawl onto the bed." I commanded. She put her hands out in front of her, feeling for the edge of the bed. Once she found it, she got on all fours and crawled her way to the middle. "Lay on your stomach." She did as she was told, laying her cheek against the comforter. I went to the side of the bed to get the handcuffs I had that were linked to the bed frames. These kept her arms secured, but out of my way. I handcuffed her left wrist to the left front bed frame, and went to the other side to cuff her other wrist.
"Now put that ass up for me." I told her. She struggled trying to lift her ass up, without the help of her arms. I went to grab the paddle from the closet. "Ten smacks… One smack for each of the 6 minutes I had to wait for

you." I took my blazer off, stood at the edge of the bed and rolled my sleeves up. She bit her bottom lip, anticipating that I was going to smack her with my hand.

I reached my arm back as if I was about to hit a baseball. As soon as the paddle hit her ass, she jerked. "Shit!" she exclaimed. I knew it hurt. I needed it to hurt. I hit her again, just as hard as the first time. "Damnit!" She yelled again.

"That was 2. We have 8 more." I reminded her. *Smack! Smack! Smack!...* Each time the paddle touched her skin, she put her ass higher in the air, waiting for the next hit. I didn't make the last five hurt as bad as the first five, but I still made sure they stung. After hearing her moan, I wasn't sure which one of us enjoyed those hits more.

"You okay?" I asked her.

"Oh yesss, daddy." She mumbled.

"Good, now keep that ass in the air." I walked to the closet to retrieve a toy we purchased together. I loved using her gadgets on her. They didn't get the job done as easily or as quickly as my dick did, but I knew exactly how to angle them inside her to get the response I wanted. Looking at her from the side had me dying to get inside. I walked up to her and kissed her on her backside. She arched her back like a kitten. I put the toy down for a second to rip her pantyhose apart from her crotch to the top of her ass. I got behind her to taste that sweet spot from the back. Her taste was so addictive. I licked from her spot, up to her ass and up her back, stopping right before the back of her neck. She moaned deeply. I rubbed the head of the toy on her clitoris. Her hole contracted, wanting to feel its depth. I slid it inside slowly, as I kissed her lower back. Her mouth was wide open, whispering obscenities. I angled the toy downward, wanting to hit her magic place. She clenched up, biting her bottom lip and rocking back on my hand. My arm movements were smooth and my stroke was direct. I pumped it inside of her as if it was me. I could picture myself in my head, deep in her womb. I looked up at her, with her tongue on the roof of her mouth. I pushed deeper, stretching her insides. She grabbed the comforter and lowered her ass onto the bed. She could always take it deeper when she was laying flat on her stomach.

"Mmm daddy..." She moaned.

"Right there?" I asked her, watching her love faces. She replied with a moan between her clenched teeth. I could tell I was hitting that magic place because I could feel her walls clenching onto the toy, making it harder to push in. She was about to cum. I hurried her by licking her ass as I pushed the toy inside her. Mouth wide open, she let out a high pitched moan, signaling the eruption. Her legs bent and knees buckled, blocking my arm from moving the way I wanted to.

"Put your legs down." I commanded. She was so far into her orgasm that she didn't respond. "Legs down!" I said firmly. She put them down for a moment but put them back up again. I had something for that. I pulled the toy out slowly and placed it on the dresser. "If you won't keep your legs down voluntarily, I will make you keep them down." I said to her, bringing out the bed cuffs I had for her ankles. They were just like the ones I had for her wrists. These connected to the bottom of the bed frame. I put them on her impatiently, and forcefully. I was about to give her what I know she wanted. She lifted her head up, completely helpless and unable to move or see, trying to hear what I was going to do next. I took my pants and shoes off, leaving my shirt on. I climbed onto the bed behind her and pushed her legs together, pulling her pantyhose down to her knees. I put my legs on the outside of hers and started to grind on her ass. She pushed back against me.

"How does it feel?" I asked, hard dick rubbing between her cheeks.

"Good, daddy."

I leaned onto my elbows to kiss her shoulders and moved her hair to lick the back of her neck furiously. She tilted her head down, giving me as much skin as possible to devour. When I licked the back of her neck, it put an automatic arch in her back.

"Put it in, please daddy." She whispered to me, whimpering.

I grabbed her hair in my hand and pulled it back, lifting her head off the bed. I put my mouth to her ear. "Don't fucking tell me what to do." I said to her. I put my other hand under her chest and up to her throat, lightly choking her while I put her earlobe in my mouth. She moaned harder. I continued to rub my dick onto her backside, rubbing the precum out of it. Finally I decided to slide it inside. It aimed for her wetness without me having to aim it with my hand. I clenched my hand tighter around her throat as I entered her. I could hear her pussy talking to me, telling me to so as deep as possible. I let go of her throat and took the blindfold off of her. She tried to look back but couldn't position herself enough to do so because of her chains. Defeated, she put the side of her face down on the bed and took my strokes.

"Did you want it this deep?" I whispered.

"Yeeessssss, daddy."

I dug orgasms out of her like I was searching for treasure. One right after the other... Each time, I changed my angle and my tempo. And each time she begged me to stop but I wouldn't. Her orgasms took the energy out of her. I wanted to wear her ass out. Two orgasms turned into 5 quickly

"I can't take anymore." She moaned to me, exhausted and panting heavily.

"What did you say?" I asked, wanting the proper response.

"Please... Daddy."

"One more..." I said bringing the front of my torso down to lay against her back.

"Damnit, Marcus." She said shaking her head. I smiled. She wouldn't let me cum when she had control. And now I wouldn't let her stop cuming. I put my hands under her breasts, squeezing them while I pounded her. She yelled sentences I couldn't understand. "Marc-uuu---shhhh--

oooo-Mmmm--Suhhh-aahhh..." Her gibberish let me know her mind was in another place. Between that and the sound of her water splashing against my dick, I was about to cum myself.
"Come on baby..." I prodded her. She put her face into the sheets, crying out. Her arms grabbed for things that weren't there. I felt her tense up. Her insides clenched around me. I couldn't hold it in anymore. I tensed up along with her. I waited to feel the contractions of her walls having another orgasm, before I allowed myself to cum. Once I felt it, I came inside of her, then I collapsed on her back. She let out a few more silent moans, allowing her body to relax.
I reached up to undo the cuffs from her wrists. They had a release lever that didn't require a key. She was so exhausted that she didn't even move her arms. I laid on top of her for several minutes, not wanting to move. When I finally decided to get up, I released her ankles from their hold. She didn't move.
"You okay baby?" I asked her. She began breathing deeply, signaling the sound of getting put to sleep. She was out for the count, laid out in the shape of an X, on her stomach, almost snoring. I laughed quietly before I went to the bathroom to wipe myself off. Daddy wore her ass out just like he planned to. The perfect TKO.

Busting Ink

Poet,
I heard your stanzas loud and clear,
They say,
when your reality becomes better than your dreams,
you'll stop getting them wet
with the thought of me.
I know you've replayed in your head
What my Brazilian waxes taste like.
How easily your tongue rides the smoothness of missing hair follicles,
How my pussy juices might actually
Water taste buds into blooming,
Only to become addicted to my perfectly
PH balanced beard fertilizer....
Let me tell you...
As a Queen of this Freakdom,
Your threats do not scare me.
Tell me,
How deep is your stroke sleep?
Like, how many slapping sounds does it take
To make my eyes roll into a coma,
Sleeping beauty-like,
Only to be awaken by the sweetest kiss on my clitoris,

See... this is why i don't mess with poets because,
I can tell that your vocabulary contains words,
That will make my pussy spit for you just
From the vibrations of your syllables,
So Tell me...
What is your safe word?
Because I plan to wrap rope
Around your wrists with the same tightness
As my lips around your dick,
These dimples mean, my cheeks can grip.

Place your thumb and finger in each,
to adjust your comfort levels,
Until the ink from your pen slides down my chin,
Writing "damn, you win" in cursive....
Because if you think I can't match your nasty,
Then you're in for a battle even the Avengers couldn't
save you from.

Now, have you ever been rode with such intensity
That you can see the name of our future kids?
Ass plopping into your pelvis as you envision each letter,
B...R...
I... will fuck you into a prophecy
No religion could foreshadow.
Make you say grace before eating cuz,
This is what heaven tastes like.
I can make you crave me so
Desperately that you will want to lick anything I touch
I admit...
That ever since I heard
Those words spill from your lips,
I've been fantasizing about you in Limericks,
And if you stroke anywhere near as
Gracefully as you speak then,
Our sex would be poetry between sheets,
Your body as chiseled as your mind,
As sharp as your words,
And I'd love to have you slice me down the middle....

I...
Not only want you to write your secrets on the back of my
throat,
And swallow,
I want your dreams to creampie into my womb,
Make no mistake,
This is not some infatuated fan speaking.
I'm an observant Queen,
That can hear the heaviness of your mind and your dick
from the stage

And this castle,
Has been lonely with cobwebs
And echoes in hallways but
Your tone is like keys to my chastity belt.
I'm not sure if this is lust or love at first listen
But my thighs and I are spread eagle to
Exploring the possibility
Of me doing a curtsy on your face before the end of the night.
So... King
You 5 minutes to decide, whether you want
To fuck me with words or your body.
The jewels of our crowns hot- bling,
In Unison that we should do both.
But just know,
That if you continue jizzing sentences like this in my ear,
The mic won't be the only thing open for you tonight.

Reunited

It had been 3 months since my baby Tasha had seen her father and her sister. Victor and I had been separated for 6 months, before his job sent him packing to Miami. I was still hurt and upset that our seven year marriage had failed. I felt like it was my fault for taking advantage of his pushover ways, and not being able to let my guard down with him. Even after marriage, I was constantly afraid of saying exactly how I felt. Since he left, it seemed like I couldn't get my life back on track. I missed him. He was such an amazing father. He still paid for Tasha's needs, and spoiled her absolutely rotten. When she would stay with him every other weekend, she would come home with a new toy to add to her already overflowing toy chest. She was clearly a daddy's girl and it warmed my heart every time I saw them together.

It was the beginning of June and Victor and I decided it would be a good idea for Tasha to spend a month out of the summer with him. So I packed up the car, and all the toys I could fit, and drove her down to see her daddy. On the drive to Miami, Tasha was surprisingly calmer than usual. I figured it was because of the allergy medicine I'd given her earlier. Just like her mother, she suffered from allergies every year and had the worst snotty nose a child could have. She asked a hundred questions: "Where are we going?" "Is Nadia gonna be there?" "Is daddy gonna be there?" "Did you get my barbies?" "Can daddy get me more barbies?"- it was never ending. Luckily she fell asleep 2 hours into the 5 hour drive, and didn't wake until we arrived.

We pulled up to Victor's townhome and Tasha immediately sat up with excited wide eyes. "Is that where daddy lives?" she asked.

"Yes baby. He lives in that blue one right there."
"That's pretty mommy."
"Yes it is, honey."
I got out the car and walked to her side to get her out. She was still sleepy but insisted on walking herself up the stairs to knock on her daddy's door. Nadia opened the door before she could even reach the top of the stairs and met her with the biggest hug, picking Tasha off the ground.
"Hey Nadia!" I yelled, embracing her while she held her sister.
"Hey miss Alicia. I'm glad you guys made it!"
Nadia seemed relieved we were there. Probably just happy to see familiar faces. She was only 10 but it seemed like she grew a few more inches in the 3 months I hadn't seen her. She was surely going to be tall, just like her father. Victor appeared at the bottom of the stairs with a huge grin.
"Is that my Tasha baby?" He asked, with a surprised, almost cartoonish facial expression.
"Daddy!" she yelled, running and jumping into his arms.
I wasn't sure what he'd been doing since he moved but my goodness his body seemed more muscular. I mean he always managed to stay in shape but his arms looked like cannons. His hair was cut and he had grown a goatee. He looked... happy. Happy and healthy. It gave me mixed emotions because I wasn't sure if this was a result of him being done with me or some decision he had made to help him get a new chick.

Victor's job paid for his moving expenses and set him up in a small, but lovely townhome on a property they owed. It was a nice set up. As long as Tasha had her own room I was satisfied. When Victor finally put her down, he asked Nadia "Can you take Tasha upstairs so she can see her new room?"
"Yes sir." She replied, holding Tasha's hand as they hurried upstairs. Then he turned to me, with a soft grin and rubbed his beard.
"So you're not going to hug me?"

I smirked. "I wasn't sure if you wanted me to."
"I mean, it has been 3 months since I've seen you, Alicia."
I thought for a second. Then looked at his charming expression and reluctantly gave in to his request... He embraced me with his arms over mine and my hands wrapped around his waist. He smelled so good. I wanted to put my nose in the crevice of his neck but I knew that wasn't a good idea. I could tell the difference in his grip. It was stronger. He had definitely been working out... hard. It felt like we had been holding each other forever. I tried not to think too much about what it meant. Victor was always an affectionate person but we hadn't hugged like that since... Well, it had been a while. When he pulled away from me, he looked in my face, with his hands still touching me, softly gripping my arms and said "I'm really glad you both made it safely."
"Me too. And thanks for inviting me." I replied.
"No problem... Do you want any coffee or anything?" he asked walking into the kitchen. "I know it's early in the evening but I know you love your coffee and tea."
I walked into his living room. "No. Water is fine."
"I also made some lemonade this morning. It's really good," he yelled.
"Okay, I'll take the lemonade."
"Good choice!"
This was weird. Since we separated, whenever I brought Tasha over, we would just have small talk, I'd say goodbye to Tasha and I'd leave. Most of the time I never even set foot in that apartment. Now I was inside his home and had to stay the night. I hoped I stayed on my best behavior. Suddenly his house phone rang. Worried it was another female, my nosey ass listened in on the conversation.
"Hello?... hey! What's going on? ... (laugh) yea Tasha just got here. She's upstairs with Nadia... Of course!... When?... okay... Oh really? (laugh again).... Well yea, I'll definitely be available for that.... Okay... Well I'll have to

talk with you about it later, I'm a little busy right now.... Great... Okay bye."

I hoped it wasn't a girlfriend, or sex buddy or anybody he had moved on with. I wondered if he had met someone in Miami in the short amount of time he had been there. Why didn't he tell the person I was here? Was I not important? I was too proud to ask any of those questions. We were separated, so it wasn't my business but that didn't stop the thoughts.

"Here you go." He said, handing me my glass of lemonade.

"Thanks."

We sat there. Awkwardly listening to the news channel. Wanting to have more of a conversation but not knowing what to say. I tried to think of something to break the ice.

"How's Cicely?" I hated his mother but I figured it would drown the silence.

"She's good! She actually seeing a white guy now."

"What? Black Power Cicely?"

"Yep. I don't know what he did or said but she is absolutely in love with this guy. Crazy isn't it?" he said chucking.

I began laughing almost uncontrollably. "As much junk as she talked about interracial couples and the white man being the oppressor, she's now dating one? Wow! I'm shocked!"

"We're all shocked!"

"Wow... When did she meet him?"

"Sometime last year. She managed to keep it a secret until Aunt Karen found out and let the cat out of the bag."

"Wow. Good 'ol Cicely. I have to give her props on that one. That's one thing you rarely see, a white man and a black woman... Especially an older couple." I was glad I asked about her. That was probably the news of the year for me, something I ever expected. "How do you like him?"

"He's cool. He's a nice guy and he treats my mother like a queen. I have no problems with him at all. If she's happy, I'm happy." He smiled and I smiled with him, happy black power Cicely had broadened her horizons. I asked him more about other family members, his sisters, his uncle, a couple of his cousins. Time seemed to get away from us while we cracked jokes and got caught up on the past year. Talking like this with him aroused me. Reminded me of being in our home acting like college students. How we would go from a conversation, to a disagreement, to me kissing his cheeks while apologizing for upsetting him, to passionate sex. I looked at his jeans when I could and wondered if it was still mine. If anybody else had the pleasure if sitting on something so powerful, while we weren't together.

Meanwhile, we could hear the loud footsteps of the girls upstairs playing. I called out them. "Nadia! Tasha!!!" They didn't respond; too entertained by whatever game they were playing. I got up, stood by the stairs and called them again. Still no response, but the footsteps and laughing continued.

"You can go upstairs if you want. Nothing up there is going to get you, I promise" he joked.

I gave him a side eye, rolled my eyes playfully and walked upstairs to Nadia's room where I heard the girls playing. I opened the door and found them both jumping on and off the bed in princess costumes.

"Girls?"

"Yes mommy?" Tasha said climbing back on to bed.

"You guys are making too much noise. Calm it down a little bit okay?"

"Yes ma'am." Nadia said, almost out of breath.

"Hey mommy, come look at my room!" Tasha said, sprinting off the bed, landing on the floor and zooming past me across the hall into her room. "Look! Daddy got me a car for my Barbies!"

I gasped. "Really? Can you fit them all in there?"

"Yes! There are one... two... three... four seats and I have one... two... three... four barbies!"

"That's awesome Tasha! Make sure you tell daddy thank you before you go to bed, okay?"

"Yes ma'am."

"Okay, make sure you guys keep it down too!" I yelled before walking into Victor's room. I figured I'd give myself a tour, since he didn't give me one. It was large, with a high sitting King size bed. I walked over to it and looked carefully at the pillows for signs of lipstick or foundation. I tried not to move anything around too much, so he wouldn't be suspicious that I was snooping around. I found nothing. He had a spacious walk in closet and a bathroom that had a separate bathtub and shower. I definitely didn't expect a bathroom this fancy from him, since he was such a simple guy. I stood at his sink, then looked at myself in the mirror. Making sure desperation wasn't written on my face. I looked at his sinks carefully, searching for any trace of an abnormally long hair strand. I peeped into his trash can looking for any panty liners or tampons, but was interrupted by sound of Victor's voice.
"You know, if I did have a woman here and I was trying to hide it, I could've simply emptied the trash can so there would be no trace of her."
With my hand on my chest, I responded, "You scared the hell outta me."
"Is that what you were looking for?"
"What?"
"Something another woman may have left behind?"
"No! I was... just... looking at everything. This is a really big bathroom. And its really nice"
"You can ask me if I've been seeing someone. I'm not going to get defensive or judge you or any of that."
"It's really none of my business."
"That doesn't mean you aren't still curious about it."
I paused and took a deep breath. "Have you been... seeing anyone?"
"No. Honestly, I haven't been able to really give anyone that type of attention since we... separated."
I wanted to say *Me too* but I was too afraid to admit how I felt. I was never good at expressing myself at the appropriate times. "Okay" I said, hoping he didn't try to penetrate deeper.
"You aren't going to ask me about sex?"

That word startled me. "What do you mean?"
"Like, you're not going to ask me if I've been physical with anyone?"
"Wouldn't that count as seeing them?"
"Not necessarily."
I wanted to know the answer so bad. It killed me to ask. He could see the struggle on my face. "Have you?"
"Yes."
My heart dropped. We had been separated but that wasn't something I was prepared to hear. I guess I assumed since I wasn't, that he wasn't either.
"One time?"
"A few times..."
"Okay." I had so many questions after that but I was sure I didn't want to know the answers. "Well thanks for being honest."
"What about you?" He asked. I should've seen that coming. Maybe he was being honest with me, because he wanted me to come clean too. But there was nothing to come clean about.
"No." I responded shaking my head. "Nobody. Not even sex."
He nodded. We sat there for a moment soaking this conversation in. I wanted desperately not to think about what he did with her when they slept together. So I tried to dig myself out of my feelings.
"I see you've been working out."
He chuckled "Yea... I was under a lot of stress. So I hit the gym hard. It was either that or sticking my dick in someone. Well, other than the one chick. She was nothing like you are in bed. So that will never be anything more than what it was..."
"She wasn't like me, huh?"
"Nope. Not even close."
At this point I was curious and flattered that he held my love making skills on such a pedestal. I flipped my hair behind my shoulder. "And what was I like?"

He grinned, showing those gorgeous white teeth. "You were an animal. Having me twisted around your finger every time you said my name."

My panties got moist hearing him say that. I had never asked him before how I was in bed. But I knew our sex was always brilliant.

He continued, "You have this hunger in your eyes. It's like you always wanted me to give you more."

I interjected, "-And you always gave me more. I loved that.."

"Loved? You say that in the past tense. You wouldn't still love it?"

My nipples hardened. I licked my lips. He took that as an invitation to come taste them. I leaned against the sink and he put both of his hands beside me, pushing his hardness against me. He put his lips close to my face and waited for my lips to agree to reconnect. He always had the softest lips... I brushed my nose against his, and kissed him lightly at first. Trying to take him in doses. I feared if I devoured his mouth like I wanted to, I'd lose complete control. And I did. After the fourth kiss, I wanted it all, everything I had been missing. Everything he took away when he packed his things to leave. I missed it. I yearned for it. I needed it all. He picked me up and sat me on the sink, remembering where every button was that he could push, licking my neck until I surrendered... Until I pulled his manhood out of his pants and rubbed it against the crotch of my panties. Wearing my maxi dress always meant easy access... Then we heard Tasha crying. We tried to continue, but she called out my name. Victor kissed me slowly once more, and then stepped back to let me tend to her. I was weak. My mind was on cloud 10 but mommy duties were never ending. .

I strolled into her room, slowly. Apparently she had jumped off her bed and hit her head on the side of her dresser somehow. She had acquired a small cut on her forehead. I cleaned it, put Neosporin on it, put a Band-Aid over it and gave her a bath. It was almost her bedtime and she was becoming silly from sleepiness. Victor went to get our bags out the car and I got her dressed and ready for bed. He and I sat on our knees beside her bed and prayed with her, like we did before the separation. I never told him, but while Tasha said her prayers, I prayed that this was a sign that we would get back together. I prayed that I found the courage to tell him I was sorry for mistreating him and causing the crack that eventually split us apart.

After making sure Nadia and Tasha were both comfortably in their beds, Victor and I went downstairs into the kitchen and laughed about past memories we had made together. I sat at the island watching him cater to me, making me some tea and putting the exact amount of sugar and lemon I liked in it, just like he did before the separation. I wanted to bring up what happened in his bathroom but I didn't want to force anything. I wasn't sure when the right time was to discuss what I was feeling. We'd had such a great evening. I didn't want to ruin anything. But Victor could always read me like a book.

"What's wrong?" he asked, while stirring his tea.

I didn't even look up at him. "Nothing."

"Alicia." He called out. I looked up and stared blankly at him, trying to make sure he couldn't read anything I was feeling. "What is it? Talk to me."

"It's nothing... Really."

"No, It's something, definitely."

I paused and exhaled. "Vic, I really don't want to mess this moment up. We have had a great night."

"Yes we have, and it could be better if you would just stop trying to hide how you feel all the time."

My eyes began to water. I put my hands over my face and forced myself to say what I needed to say.

"I'm sorry, for everything. I'm sorry we're even here right now. We shouldn't even be here. We should be having this discussion in OUR home, that WE shared together, not in your home." The tears began to fall. "I know this was all my fault. I'm not an easy person to deal with and I'm sorry. I've purposely made this hard on you because I wasn't willing to sacrifice my pride for us. I never wanted this to happen. I didn't think you would leave but I'm almost glad that you did, because I wouldn't have realized how wrong I was if you hadn't. I feel like such a failure as a wife, and a person. I can't believe I let the best thing that ever happened to me, leave like that. And had so much pride that it took almost a year to ask you to come back. I'm sorry and I miss you so much..."

He sat there soaking it all in. "So you're asking me to come back?"

"Yes. I'm begging you to come back."

He was silent, not sure what to say. He wasn't prepared for that. I had never admitted my wrongs to him that way.

He asked me if I was done with my tea, and I was confused. "You're not going to say anything about what I just said?"

"I don't know what to say, Alicia. I was actually hoping you would apologize but I didn't think you would. And I certainly didn't think you would ask me to come back. I'm stunned."

I was overcome with the need for answers. "So do you think we can repair this?"

"I don't know. We would need to have a plan of action, some way to make sure you were really trying to change for us."

"I'll do whatever you need me to do, Victor. I really want my family back."

Nodding his head, he took my cup and washed it out with his in the sink. "So ummm... I just put fresh sheets on my bed. You can lay there and I'll sleep on the couch. It gets cooler down here with the air on, so I figured you'd be more comfortable up there."

I felt defeated. I thought he would be more receptive to my outpour of emotions. I thought he would be happy and proud of me. Instead he seemed detached all of a sudden.

"No, I can sleep down here. This is your house. I don't want to take your bed away."
"No Alicia, I'm sleeping down here. Trust me the bed is much more comfortable."
I was pissed, so I let out a deep sigh and walked hurriedly to his room, worried that I would burst into tears if I asked him anything else. I lay awake for two hours. Picturing 50 different ways this trip could have gone if I had just kept my mouth shut. Wondering if I should have stayed at a hotel in the first place.

Then my hormones took over. I became anxious, stressed, and horny at the same time. I tried not to touch myself but being in his bed had me yearning for him. I got up, still in my bra and panties and crept down the hall. put my ear to the girls rooms to make sure they were asleep. Nothing. He was laying on his couch asleep on his stomach with the TV on. I climbed quietly on top of him and whispered in his ear. "Victor, baby." He didn't move. So I kissed him on the cheek and along his jawline until he shifted. "Baby?"
"Hmm?" he responded.
"You awake?"
"Mm hmm"... He replied with his eyes closed. I began to kiss him on his back, making sure I licked down his spine to wake him up more. He moaned. I went to kiss the back of his neck and he called my name out softly.
"Alicia..."
"Yes baby?"
"You're going to wake the girls up."
"Well, I guess we just have to be quiet then, don't we?" I said, kissing down to his ass cheeks and the back of his thighs. He let out deep sigh, after deep sigh, letting me know it was okay to continue.
"I want you to look at me, baby." I said to him, waiting for him to turn over to face me... I looked into his eyes and straddled him, then Leaned over and kissed him deeply. He wrapped his arms around me, stroking my back and squeezing my ass. My camel toe rubbed against his dick in his basketball shorts and I began to moan

quietly. He took my breasts out of my bra and sucked my nipples gently. Which sent tingles shooting through my clitoris, and heightened the sensation of me rubbing against his dick. I could feel myself about to cum. He had his tongue on one breast, one hand squeezing the other breast, and one hand inside my panties, playing with my ass while I rubbed against him. That climax was so intense that my bottom jaw began to shake, as if I had chills. I came all in my panties but he also had a wet spot on his shorts where my pussy had been. I felt like putty in his hands.

"I'm sorry Victor. I love you, baby...." I moaned to him before taking my panties and his shorts off.

"Show me." He responded, grinning, with his fingers interlocked in mine. I pulled him up by his hands, positioning him with his back against the couch and his feet on the floor. I kissed him passionately, knowing it might be the last time. I held him in my hand and eased myself on to his thickness. It had been over 9 months since we'd had sex. My pussy had practically closed itself up, so getting him in my door again was beautifully painful. I threw my arms around his neck and squeezed each time I inched down on him. He grabbed my hips and pushed me down onto him forcefully, making me shriek loudly. He moaned once he was all the way in. It took a second for me to catch my rhythm. Getting past the first few strokes was tough, but my pussy had been molded to the shape of his dick and missed him so much that she got used to him quickly. I rode him slow and deep- trying to keep our silence so we wouldn't wake the girls. I could hear myself splashing onto him. He held me close, pushing his waist up to meet my pussy every time I slid down. This was pure ecstasy; cupping the back of his head in my hands and feeling him bite my shoulder. He looked up at me and bit his bottom lip. I could see something in his eyes that let me know he missed me, even though he wouldn't say it. I was sucked into the moment, even forgetting where I was momentarily. He slid out further on the couch, making me lean forward. He grabbed both of my ass cheeks in his hands and proceeded to slam me down onto him. I could feel the shift in our energies. We went from me saying I was sorry, to him accepting my apology, physically. And accepting meant marking his territory again, inside of me. He wrapped his arms around my back, and pumped into me from underneath. I began moaning loudly, with the same volume as the slaps of my ass against his thighs. He stroked me harder and harder, until I cursed.

"Shit, baby..." I moaned.

"You miss me?" He asked.

"Yessssss."

"You miss this dick?"

"Mmm hmmm."

"What?"

"Yesssss!"

"You want me back?"

"Yes, Victor..." I whined.

"Say it."

"Come back, baby."

"I can't hear you."

"Shit!" I could feel him in my stomach, pounding and stabbing my insides.

"What you say?"

"Please... Please... Come... back to me." I said, between thrusts. I didn't give a damn about waking the girls up by that time. I wanted my husband back. Victor never told me to be quiet either, taking advantage of my vulnerable state. My eyes began to roll back. I threw my head back, riding the wave of the orgasm he was hammering out. I felt my walls contract, and felt my insides get more moist than usual. We were cuming together. He was releasing inside of me. It was a feeling I'd taken for granted while we were together, and one I planned on appreciating more. It was warm, and so rewarding that I didn't want him to leave my womb. We kissed, with me sucking on his tongue until he got completely soft. Even then, I wouldn't let him outside of me. With my hands rubbing his chest, I looked into his eyes and asked, "What happens now?" halfway afraid of his response. He spread his arms out on the back of the couch and took a deep breath.

"What happens now... Is you go back upstairs." He said, coldly. My heart dropped. This wasn't what I had expected after that kind of love making. It was all too much for me. I had apologized enough. There was nothing more I could do. I got off of him slowly, picking up my panties off the floor, and started walking up the stairs.

"Alicia." He called out. I looked over at him, holding my breath. "I'll be up in a minute." He said, grinning.

I gave a sigh of relief and laughed quietly. I almost thought the makeup session meant nothing. Now that I was able to put my pride aside, we would be able to work on us.

"Okay baby." I replied. "I'll be waiting for you."

The Reconstruction

5'5" Godiva Chocolate bar,
Hair, that curls with the shape of her thoughts,
Forever spinning,
Forever wrapped around rod's
Of mysterious fingertips
That massage the anxiousness of her mind,
Freshly pedicured feet that
Are tired from walking across the surface of uncertainty,
Arms that embrace skin like sun,
Thighs that shake like quiet storms when
Uncertain...

6'2" Almond milk,
Eyes, that calm even the most restless of spirits,
Hands, that were made to build stability,
Wrists, that could martial arts their way
Into any crevice his mind couldn't penetrate,
His legs could lift the stresses off of any woman
Carrying them...

Stares
Waiting for each other to make move,
He looks at her as if she is skyscraper that needs
Remodeling,
She looks at him, as if he is construction crew
They arrive bare...
Stripped of all their clothing,
She allows him on her property,
He palms the nape of her neck as if he is
Reading her floor plan,
He's ready to mix pleasure with business.

Kisses

Carefully placed around her wiring,
Sucking honey from her glands
Tracing patterns to her generator,
Knowing water is dangerous when mixed with electricity,
So he cleans her with his mouth,
Finding where her weaknesses lie,
Vacuuming out her heartaches
And swallowing anything that doesn't belong there,
Pressure washing her
So intensely that her juices make his lips glisten,

Hands
Treating her body like braille,
He says "show me where it hurts"
And She responds with chill bumps,
Anywhere she needs his mouth to be bandaid,
Stretch marks that make the blind wish they could see her melanin,
His arms under her back, holding her steady,
Fixated, on putting dynamite in her basement,
She's shaking, anticipating detonation,
He knows her structure must be reaffirmed from the inside out...

Chaos.
Everything around her falling,
Breaking,
Bombs going off inside her tunnels,
Lungs collapsing,
Moans sounding like Sirens,
He holds her hands,
To make sure she doesn't disrupt
The rearranging of steel,
Jackhammering his way into her soul,
This part would not be pretty,
Her love faces resemble broken concrete,
Groaning
heavy, Long and deep as if she is in mourning,
Grieving,

Every stressful moment she had is leaving,
Every bad decision being compressed,
Sentences that sound like static on radio waves,
Yet he can still hear her body's requests,
He is lithium battery,
He won't stop, until she has been completely dismantled,
Her orgasms appear in her tear ducts,
She is crying
Not because she's in pain,
But because he is in tune,
Disrupting her emotional suffering with
medicine that is hard to take...
He kisses her feet,
Tells her to stop running from his love,
Slides his tongue across her arches
While he strokes the name of the last man
Out of her memory...
He wraps himself around her body,
she feels like she has been mummified
feels like Egyptian royalty,
King and Queen revel in the riches of their transparency,
she pays him in curse words that
Let him know his hard work is paying off...

Calm
The slow rise and fall of chests
Both trying to catch breath,
Trying to match the other's rhythm,
She finds peace.
Someone who understands how to fit in her formation,
Fingers Interlocked
Because these towers looks like restoration,
Like new beginnings,
Like sometimes,
You have to succumb to deconstruction,
So you can have your happy ending...

Getting out the Friendzone

"Gabby!" Brandon's mom yelled at me with open arms. I hadn't seen Mrs. Clark since My Junior year in College. I was thankful Brandon and I had remained best friends for 10 years. My family had moved to New York a year ago, and I simply didn't feel like flying into those winter storms for Thanksgiving. So I cancelled my ticket at the last minute and decided to spend my time with the Clarks. Brandon's family was always my second family.
"Gabby! It's so good to see you! You look amazing!" Mr. Clark said hugging me.
"Yea, it's crazy what fear of diabetes can do!" I said, referencing my weight loss.
"Tell me about it. Me and the misses are on a diet right now. Well, except for today", he said chuckling.
I walked into their enormous home, and said hello to the other family members, including Brandon's younger sister, 3 of his aunts, two of his uncles and 3 cousins. I was in awe at the Christmas decorations that were already up. "Mrs. Clark, you really outdid yourself this time." I said, admiring the huge tree in the living room, the holiday frames around all the pictures and the Christmas lights lining the staircase.
"Oh this is nothing. You should've been here last year!"
"I tell ya," Mr Clark added, "She really 'Turnt up' last year." he said, quoting the term with his hands. I burst into laughter. "Turnt up" was a phrase my generation created, which was another way of saying someone "Got excited" or "Got hype." I was so tickled.
"Mr. Clark, you are not allowed to say that in my presence." I said laughing.
He laughed with me. "Listen, I can still hang!" he said, high fiving me. Mrs. Clark rolled her eyes and smiled. "Let

him get your bags and take them to your room. You have the last one on the hall."
I handed him my bags and asked Mrs. Clark about Brandon.
"Oh, he's in the basement. I didn't tell him you were coming." Mrs. Clark said grinning.
"What? Why?"
"Because I forgot. It was last minute and I was busy trying to get the food and decorations. He'll be fine. It's not like ya'll don't talk to each other all the time anyway." She said, making her way to the kitchen. "You want anything to drink? We have some imported Rum, Grey Goose, red wine, beer... We also have some sodas in here if you want any." I always thought Brandon had the coolest parents on earth. They were never too good to have a drink with you.
"What about water?"
"Is Deer park fine?"
"Yes ma'am!" I said, grabbing it from her. "Let me make my way to the basement and say hi to this fool." I said, heading down to see Brandon. We talked often but I hadn't seen him since my weight loss.
I opened the basement door and went down into the dimly lit space. It was cool down there but not as cold as I had anticipated. Brandon must've had a heater on. Once I got to the bottom I looked over at him sitting in a chair, shuffling through boxes.
He called out to me, not looking back, thinking I was his mother. "Hey ma, Do you mind if I take some of these albums with me back home?"
"You'd have to ask your mom that." I replied. He turned to look at me.
"Gabby? What the hell are you doing here?" He said, grinning and getting up to hug me.
"There's a storm in NY, so I didn't have a choice but to come here. You know I've missed you guys."
He stepped back from hugging me and looked me up and down. "Where did all the meat go?" He asked.

"Don't be a jerk Brandon." I replied hitting him on the shoulder. He laughed.
"No, I mean, I knew you lost weight but you know I like meat. I'm just tryna figure out where it went so I can go get it and put it back on you."
"You don't think I look good?"
"Don't get me wrong, you look... You look great. I'm just not used to you like this. That's all" he said, chuckling.
"Well get used to it." I said playfully. He nodded stared at me for a second, looking me up and down. How awkward.
"You looking at photos?" I asked him,.
"Uhhh, yea. I was looking at the stuff from our senior year in high school. All the pictures from the football games and all of that. Pictures of you cheering. Pictures from us all going Ice skating that time..." He pulled out the ice skating pictures.
"Oh yea I remember that! You fell so many times that day!"
"Yea I busted my ass and ya'll clowned me."
"Yea, 'cause you were talking shit before we got there, acting like you were gonna master ice skating in 5 minutes. You couldn't even stay off your ass for five minutes."
"So now who's the asshole." He said snatching the pictures from me. We laughed. "Oh, look at our prom night. I can't believe you went with Chuck Newman of all people."
"He was so sweet. He asked me like a complete gentleman so I had to go with him."
"I asked you!."
"You didn't ask me. We were playing PlayStation and you were like 'Hey Gab, we should go to the prom together and show out.' That's not asking me."
"But I still asked."
"Whatever. Plus going with you would've been like going with my brother."
Brandon paused and looked at me.
"So I'm like... a Brother."

I stared at him... "I mean, we've been friends for 10 years... I mean... Maybe not a brother but... At that time it would have been weird, you know?"
"Hmm." He replied, not sure what to say. "Well, I think it's getting close to dinner time. We should probably head upstairs." I wanted to say more but I decided maybe the conversation was better left where it was.
"Okay, sure. It smells good up there."
We walked up into the kitchen to all the food on the table, ready to be devoured. We prayed and went around the table saying what we were thankful for. The Clarks were so close knit with their family, and provided more than enough food for everyone. Glazed ham, turkey, collards, mac and cheese, stuffing, cornbread, potato salad, dirty rice... My tummy was in heaven. The kids were sent upstairs and the rest of us stayed downstairs laughing and joking over drinks. Mr. Clark made sure nobody's glass was ever empty. Before I knew it, I was somewhere between tipsy and drunk, telling embarrassing stories to Brandon's Aunts about his dating life in college.
"I think you've had enough to drink." Brandon said, trying to stop my rambling mouth.
"No, I can use a couple more glasses."
"No you're done." Brandon said, taking my glass.
"Well can you bring me back a Deer Park!" I yelled at him. He chuckled and shook his head. I was never the type to drink and do crazy things that I forgot in the morning. I was completely aware that I was intoxicated and talking too much. And while it was entertaining to everyone else, Brandon felt embarrassed.
Two hours later, people started leaving, taking to-go plates with them on the way. Mrs. Clark insisted I didn't help her clean, since I was a visiting. So she, Brandon and his sister cleaned the kitchen. Mr. Clark had drank himself into passing out on the couch, and Mrs. Clark left him right there.
"He'll come upstairs sometime in the night. He'll be okay." She said referring to her intoxicated husband. "I'm

going to sleep. There are towels and extra sheets in the closet in your room, dear." She said to me.
"Thank you Mrs. Clark." I said, my eyes still glazed from the liquor.
"You're welcome honey, and drink plenty of water too! Goodnight you guys!"
She and Brandon's sister headed upstairs to their rooms. I went into my room and plopped face first on to my bed, feeling sleep approaching. Brandon knocked gently on my door, even though it was open.
"What's up?" I asked.
"I brought you some water." He said handing me the bottle.
"Thank you."
"No problem."
I looked up at him. I'm not sure if it was the liquor or the lighting in my room that made him ridiculously sexy.
I admired his body. As an athlete, he always managed to stay in shape. And I always wondered what he looked like naked but I knew that was inappropriate for our relationship. Friends shouldn't see other friends naked, right?
"What?" he said, confused by me staring.
"Nothing."
"You know you're drunk, right?"
"I'm not drunk. I'm almost drunk"
"Keep telling yourself that." He said, sitting on the bed next to me. "You almost told all of my business tonight too. I should tickle you for that."
"Awww, come on! The stories were harmless and hilarious. Don't be like that!" I said chuckling. "Plus, I've got too much alcohol in my belly for you to be tickling me."
He reached over and poked me in my stomach. I immediately started laughing and putting my hands up to guard any more attempts to tickle me. "Stop playing Brandon! Seriously." He laughed at me and shook his head. We always played around like we were still in high school when we were around each other.

"You know, times like this, I wish I had a boyfriend, so I could get thanksgiving sex right now."
"You need a boyfriend for thanksgiving sex?"
I sat up on my elbows. "Well I mean, I wouldn't be spending thanksgiving with his family if he wasn't my boyfriend."
"A friend couldn't do it?" He said looking at me, smirking.
"Well if that friend and I had sex then we wouldn't be friends anymore. We'd be more than friends."
"And what's wrong with that?"
I paused. "I don't know... I've never messed with anyone I was friends with."
"Never?"
"Never. Once you are friend zoned, that's how it stays. It's just a line I don't cross."
Brandon chuckled. "You know, some of the best relationships can happen from friendships. If you let it go there."
"If I have sex with them?"
"Maybe... But I just meant if you let one of your friends date you or something."
I laid back down and closed my eyes. The liquor had made me too sleepy for this conversation. It also made me completely oblivious to the fact that Brandon was suggesting he and I should be more than friends.
"Brandon, you're weird." I mumbled.
"Oh, am I?" He said, thumping me in my forehead.
"Ouch!" I moaned, rubbing my forehead. "...With your long ass fingers!"
"Goes perfect with your long ass forehead." He said jumping up from the bed. I tried to kick him but my legs couldn't muster up enough energy to do it fast enough.
"You're such a jerk." I blurted out.
"A jerk that you still love."
"Whatever." I said, yawning.
"Alright girl, I'm going to bed. You need anything?"
"No." I said laughing and closing my eyes again.
"Alright, I'll be across the hall if you need someone to hold your hair."

"I'm not gonna get sick B. I'm fine."

"Alright... Well goodnight." He closed my door and in five minutes, I was in la-la land.

Two hours later I woke up with a ridiculous headache, and couldn't go back to sleep. I got up and went into the bathroom to see if they had any pain killers. I grabbed the bottle of Aleve and headed to the kitchen to get some juice. Mr. Clark was still lying on the couch, snoring the night away. He was so loud I could hear him from my room. I tiptoed to the fridge to get a glass of tea and tiptoed back to my room. Then I decided that I might as well take my shower since it would be a while before the Aleve kicked in. After the shower, I laid in my bed with my bra and panties, and stared at the ceiling. My headache had gone away, thankfully, but my body started feeling tingles. I rubbed on my tummy, feeling my own warmth, and wishing it was someone else's hand... Then rubbed on the top of my vagina, playing with the thin strip of hair I left there... Then I opened up the lips and played with my clitoris. I thought about someone. Someone I cared about, touching and rubbing on me. Someone whose touch was electrical. I thought about.... Brandon. I wondered if the rumors I heard in college about his sex were true. I wondered if being physical with him would take us deeper into a real relationship with each other. He was right, nothing would be wrong if we took it there, but I was apprehensive about what would happen after.

Still in my bra and panties, I went across the hall and cracked open his door. The TV was on, creating a smooth glow on his shirtless back. He was dead asleep, laying on his stomach and hugging his pillow. I closed the door behind me and walked over to the side of the bed to look at him.

"This is ridiculous." I said to myself, walking back over to the door. I put my hand on the knob and took a deep breath. If I was going to try him, this would be the time. This was the perfect opportunity to see what could become of us. I exhaled and walked back over to the bed.

I was awkward, trying to figure out the smoothest way to climb into the bed without startling him. I decided to get under his covers with him... my pussy moist from anticipation. He shifted, turning his face towards me, still asleep. I climbed onto his back and pressed my body against his backside, waking him. He lifted his head to look at me.
"Gabby?"
"Yes." I said, confirming my presence, and kissing on his back.
"You okay?" He asked, almost confused.
"Mmm hmmm." I responded, still kissing his back. Then he became silent. I looked up, trying to see his face through the glare of the TV. His eyes were closed but he was biting his bottom lip. So I licked the middle of his back, up to the back of his neck. He began to breathe heavy, moaning in whispers. I licked his left side and he let out a quiet moan, while turning over. I straddled him, pressing my chest against his... feeling his hardness against my middle. My finger traced the outside of his jawline. My lips were half an inch away from his... We took in the moment, staring at each other, while I slowly grinded on him. Then he licked my bottom lip and pressed his lips against mine. His kisses made chills flow through my body and stop at the arches of my feet. He squeezed my thighs, rubbing his hands up to my ass, to my sides, and up my back to unhook my bra. I slipped my arms out of it and dangled my breasts in his face, wanting to feel his
tongue on them. He gave my nipples the same slow kisses he gave my lips. Knowing his dad was just outside in the living room asleep, I tried to keep my moaning to a minimum but he licked my breasts so perfectly that I had to let them out... He released my nipple from his tongue's cage to take my panties off. Our movements were like water... smooth and in tune.
"Sit on my face...." He whispered.
The way he said it made my pussy throb. I kissed him again, deeply before I followed to his command, placing

my dripping pussy over his thirsty mouth. He kissed the insides of my thighs first, taking his time. I knew there was no turning back after this moment. Once the bodily fluids started being tasted, I knew I was going all the way. I put my hand under his head and lowered myself onto his tongue. He moaned, tasting me for the first time, as I smothered his face. When I rocked back, his tongue flicked forward on my clitoris. When I rocked forward, his tongue flicked back, slowly. My eyes rolled into my head and my mouth fell open. I put my hands on the bed frame for support, as the orgasm drew near. He put his hands on my breasts and squeezed gently. My thighs shook like an earthquake. I swear he sucked my soul right through my clitoris when I came. I felt it completely leave my body and float into another realm. I looked down into his eyes

and saw him differently. It was strange, and I'd hate to say I was in love at that moment, but everything I felt about him skyrocketed. I was scared, not really knowing if my feelings were appropriate.

"You okay?" He asked me, licking his lips. I nodded my head, unsure of what to say. "You want to stop?"

"I don't know" I whispered back, still panting. I went back to my straddling position, so I could look him in his face. "What does this mean?"

"I believe this means we are taking things further. Unless you don't want to."

I stared at him. "I do."

He pulled me down to kiss him again. "We don't have to do anything else if you don't want to. I don't want to rush anything."

"But I want to..."

"You sure?"

I nodded and kissed his chin. The amount of concern he had for my comfort only made me more sure that I was choosing the right person. I smiled at him and he smiled back, knowing we were completely in tune with each other. He then rolled me over, laying me on my back, got on top of me, and proceeded to almost make me cum from licking, sucking and biting on my neck. Every nerve sent signals to my pussy, making it swell. It didn't matter where he put his mouth on me, I always felt like cumming. He took off his boxer briefs and allowed the head of his tool to rub against me. I held it in my hand and aimed it for my opening. He pushed it in softly and slowly, kissing my cheek and breathing lightly in my ear. I kissed his shoulders and his neck, occasionally gasping for air until the initial pain subsided. I put my hands on his ass and squeezed as he stroked me. He had his chest against mine, and kissed me while he caressed my insides. He whispered in my ear, telling me how good I felt; letting me know he wasn't going to stop until I came again. He made love to me like a samurai, with precision. It was slow but intense. His strokes got faster but more shallow.

"That's it baby." I moaned to him.

"Right there?"

"Mmm hmm."

His technique was unmatched. His passion was overwhelming. My heart was pounding through my chest, feeling the kind of attachment I was forming. As my orgasm came again, I put my hands on his upper back, feeling the sweat that had formed there. My breathing got shallow and erratic as I squeezed his back. He could feel me cuming and gripped my shoulders, making sure I didn't move as he dug the orgasm out of me. I was on an emotional and mental high as he stroked me through it. I could tell he was also cuming by his grunting and the loss of his rhythm. I wrapped my legs around him, making sure he didn't pull out. I wanted to feel it inside of me. He twitched hard during his release. It was clearly as intense for him as it was for me. We were both sweaty, hot, and gasping for air. He'll never admit it but I think I snatched his soul out of him that night too.

After we both cleaned up, he laid in my bed with me, stroking my back. We were both awake with our eyes closed.

"Brandon?" I called.

"hmmm?"
I opened my eyes to look at him. "Does this mean we're together now?"
He opened his eyes slightly "Hell yea, this means we're together. You made me cum inside you so we go together now."
"I didn't make you cum inside me."
"You wouldn't let me pullout. It's the same thing."
I laughed.
"Yea, you knew what you were doing." He said grinning.
I chuckled. "I know. But seriously though, are we really together?"
"Yes. Unless you don't want to be."
I smiled at him.
"Do you want to be?"
"Absolutely." I said.
"That's what I thought." He said playfully. I leaned over to kiss him and ended up making love to him again. That night we reached a new level together... We moved from friends to lovers with ease. The transition seemed natural. Because of our friendship, the love we had romantically was even deeper. I couldn't imagine falling in love with anyone else...

The Art of Eroticism

It's been a long day at work…
Your boss has been giving you hell about some spreadsheets someone else fucked up,
Your coworker has been doing everything in their power
To get you fired,
You spent your lunch on the phone with your friend,
Who was crying, because her boyfriend just broke up with her,
And didn't have time to finish your lunch,
You checked your funds
and you don't have the money to do shit until payday,
Which is in 2 more weeks.
You man invites you over.
Tells you the door will be unlocked,
Tells you he will make everything right
That he will Kiss you into amnesia,
Make you a dinner that your tongue can't refuse,
Even put a little money in your bank account for you,
You head over.
Thinking about all the positions he can
Fuck this day out of your mind, in,
Maybe, if he bends you over far enough,
The blood will rush to your head like whirlpool and
Wash away the negativity,
You get there… open the door… and find him
Stroking himself in anticipation of you…
This can go a few ways.
I know some women, who don't understand the art of eroticism,
Who's freak levels almost never leave the ground,
Who have not felt the wings of kinkiness lift their hormones into the air
Like their legs,

And would rather make him stop because,
Self-pleasure, should only be done when you're by yourself.
There are some women,
Who lack patience.
Who would immediately rush over to their lover,
And replace his hand with the warmth of her throat,
Because his chest might need protection
From the pressure of his own release,
There are some.
Who'd rather feel that same stroke inside of her,
Pull her panties to the side and ride him like
Her survival depends on how hard her bounce is...

But me...
Id pour myself a drink....
Sit on the couch opposite of him,
And watch him intensely,
As he rubs that anticipation out...
My kind of eroticism revels in the fact that,
Good things come to those who know how to watch it unfold,
I'd rub nipples through my clothes
and ask him if he can see how hard he's made them.
Who will tell him to go faster or slow down,
According to how deeply my yoni pulsates,
As i listen to him breathe,
I might, sit on his knee
and feed him my tongue,
And ask him to cum on my thighs,
I love a shooter.

Or maybe...
I will sit my ass on table like a plate of brown sugar and pineapple glazed ham,
Spread my legs, displaying the only meal that has all 3 courses in one,
make him sit there

And watch me strum his name with the tip of my finger
on places so moist,
Michael Phelps could win gold metal there,
Let's see who can hold out the longest,
Let my finger massage my middle to his rhythm,
Moans and groans speaking to each other saying,
"Damn baby, If you keep staring at me like that I'm going
To bust like nail through tire on the highway.
Might nut like Planters set up pecans and almonds inside
my labia,
I just might cum for you like my pussy was throwing
shade
At how your nasty ass couldn't wait for me..."

Or maybe, I will grab his head and tell him to
Suck on my pussy like it's a Cookout Milkshake and
My clitoris is trying to push through the circular opening
of his mouth,
Then lick myself off the thickness of his chin while he
grins.
If you've never had a man cum just from tasting the
orgasm,
He frictioned out of you,
You are missing out on a gift that will firework itself
Into your memory.
See, I don't always need dick inside me to feel full,
There are times,
When I'd rather ride the palm of your hand
Than your face.
When I'd rather be voyeur,
When I'd rather let you slide your self between the hills of
my chest
And feel the danger between my landslides,
Sometimes the spewing of warm lava against my neck
Feels better than pearls,
The best things in life are truly priceless...
but I should be able to count your deposits all over my
body...

Real pleasers are okay with not having instant gratification.
My pleasure can't be condensed into key and lock,
Sometimes, I just like to feel metal rubbing against mine without actually opening anything,
Don’t be afraid, to leave a dent on me that i can swallow,
Or that will dry up within the next 5 minutes,
Don’t get me wrong…
I love feeling the throbbing inside of me when those kids come to night care,
But when they cum outside for recess, It seems we all have a little more fun…
Don’t be so quick to get to your destination,
That you forget all the routes that you can take to get there..
Take notice of the landmarks,
Get lost on purpose
Mentally map each spot that persuades
Moans to easily slip past unsuspecting ear drums,
Take your time.
Sex might be the highlight of your vacation but
It doesn't always have to be the destination,
Be patient.
And allow this painter to introduce your brush to the true Art of Eroticism.

Those Lips

I saw him again in the Copy room. The new Division 2 supervisor. I'd seen him almost every day there for a month, since he started. He was a gorgeous Latin something. 5'9", 180lbs. I thought he was Puerto Rican at first, but he told me he was from Panama. If Panamanians looked like him, I was living in the wrong country.

"Good morning Sonya." He said with a smile.

"Good morning Alex. I'm starting to feel like you're stalking me." I joked.

"I'm not. But I can if you want me to." He joked backed, flirting. When he smiled, I just wanted to stick my tongue in his dimples. They were deep and fit his face perfectly. It also didn't help that his lips were so pink and full. Every time I saw him, I wondered what his lips felt like.

"You got any plans tonight?" he asked. It was Valentine's Day.

"Psh! I wish I had a man to go home to."

"Oh, I'm sure that's not hard for you to get."

"If it were easy, I'd have plans tonight." I said with sarcasm.

He smiled, showing his pearly whites. "I see."

I put my papers in the copier and started the printing. "What about you?"

"I'm in the same boat as you." He said.

"Come on Alex, you're an attractive guy. Getting a Valentine's date should be a breeze."

"Quality over quantity, sweetheart." He said. "I could be on several different dates tonight but the women aren't my type."

"Picky?"

"Very."

"I'm the same way, so I understand." My papers had finished their cycle through the copier. "Did you see your lips- I mean… " I stopped myself and laughed. All the fantasizing I had done about his lips became accidentally verbal. "I meant, the lists. Did you see the lists of… never mind. I messed that all up. I'm sorry."

"My lips, huh?" He said, reading me. I was so embarrassed. I had to get out of there.

"I'm sorry, I don't know why I said that." I said. I put my papers in my folder and turned to leave.

"Was that your subconscious talking?" His eyes pierced through me. His long eyelashes made his stare hard to look away from.

"I wouldn't say that" I said, feeling the tingles in my face from blushing. "I'll see you later Alex."

"I'll see you sooner." He responded, winking. I looked at him confused and then laughed it off. We were constantly flirting. The way he looked at me made it obvious that he probably was wondering how my lips felt too. And while I tried to pretend like I was unaware of his advances, I knew he could see through that. My accidental comment was the smoke signal.

Back in my office, I was working my ass off while I ate the chocolates and candies from my coworkers. I was trying not to think about the loneliness I was going to feel once I went home to my desolate bed. I hadn't had a Valentine in three years. And I hadn't felt a man's touch in almost 7 months. My plan was to go home, order a pizza, stuff my face, have some wine, masturbate, and then go to sleep. In that order. The only decision I needed to make was which toy I was going to use. I heard a knock at my office door.

"Come in!" I yelled. I just knew it was one of my new employees, asking for more work. But it was Alex.

I immediately sat up in my chair. "Oh, hey Alex." My nipples hardened.

"Hi Sonya. Are you busy?"

"No, I was just finishing up some work."

"Can I close this?" He asked pointing to the door.

"Ummm, sure. Is something wrong?"

"Nope, everything is fine." He said closing the door. He turned to look at me, and then sat one of the chairs in front of my desk. He threw his leg over his knee and locked his fingers together as if he were waiting.

"Uhh, can I help you with anything?"

"Yes you can, actually. That comment that you made in the copy room..."

"What comment?" I asked, trying to pretend like I didn't know what I'd said.

"About my lips."

I cleared my throat and looked down, embarrassed. That simple comment that slipped from my mouth, was about to get me in trouble.

"Is this about harassment?" I asked, worried he'd report it to my boss.

"Oh no." He said chuckling. "I know that was an accident. Although I'm sure you were thinking about my lips when you said it... right?"

"I was um... Errr..." I said, not wanting to admit to my mindset. Alex had me stuttering like a car losing gas. "I was just... ummm."

"It's okay. You don't have to come clean. I already know you were thinking dirty."

"How do you mean?"

He uncrossed his legs, revealing his print in his pants. I looked at it, and then looked at his face to see if he noticed I had looked at it. He definitely noticed.

"What was that you were looking at?"

"Hmm?"

"First you're talking about my lips. Now you're looking at my crotch. If I didn't know any better, I'd think you were having sex with me in your mind." His dark eyes squinted at me. He looked down at my nipples through my shirt. "It seems we both might be thinking the same thing." He added. I cleared my throat again as moisture began to form in my panties. I wanted him, and I wasn't going to deny any of his assumptions about my thoughts. He was on to me.

"It's a shame you don't have a Valentine. You are absolutely gorgeous..." He licked his lips at me. They were moist. Completely suckable.

"Thank you." I responded, blushing. I squeezed my thighs together, trying to keep more wetness from seeping through. I was nervous but he was completely calm and cool. The struggle to keep my professional composure was a serious battle.

"Do you want to know what my lips feel like?"

I wasn't sure how to answer. I kept refraining from saying yes or no. "How do you propose that happens?" I asked instead. He grinned.

"Come here."

I sat there quietly, contemplating my move. Once this started, I was sure I wasn't going to be able to stop it. He was so sexy, I couldn't help but give in. I was hoping this risk didn't end in me getting fired somehow. I got out of my chair and walked over to him, slowly.

"Closer." He commanded. I took two steps closer. "Right here." He said, pointing next to his left thigh. I stood there, looking down at him. He looked up at me and gently placed his left hand on my thigh, sliding his way up my skirt, and lifting it. Then he lifted the right side and leaned over to smell the aroma of the front of my panties, inhaling heavily. His chair sat low, but my heels also had a platform which made his face the perfect height for my middle.

"Mmm..." He moaned kissing my thighs. His lips were cool and wet. I put my hand on the back of his head, rubbing the upper part of his neck. My panties were so soaked that I knew I'd have to leave the office without them. He reached up to pull them down, doing everything as if we had all the time in the world. I slipped them off and let them lie on the floor. He put his nose in the crease of my lips, smelling again and making his dick hard as a diamond. I wanted to see that jewel. It looked so thick in his pants. He kissed me there, and I shuttered. That one kiss made my pussy throb back at him. He stuck his tongue out and slid it in the slit,

slowly... sucking when he reached my clitoris. He gave me more slow licks just like the previous, each seemed more thirsty than the one before. My juices were flowing heavily. I propped my right leg up on the back of his chair so he could get to my pearl easier.
"You taste so good, Sonya." He whispered to me. I pushed his face into me, throwing my head back from the sensations. He put his hand in between my leg and around the back of my thigh, holding me... Helping me stay balanced on my heel. I heard him unzip his pants. I looked down at him, to see what other trouble he was up to. He slipped his hand in and maneuvered around so he could pull that thick dick out. It was beautiful. He began rubbing it with his other hand, firmly. Watching him play with himself turned me on more. The sensations of his licks became intense. I put my hands on the back of his shirt collar and pulled him towards my pussy, pushing myself against his mouth. I couldn't tell if it was my juices or his saliva or the mixture of both that ran down his chin and dripped onto his shirt. I pulled away from him.
"What?" He asked me with my juices all over his chin.
"Your shirt." I said, pointing to the wet spot. I didn't want him walking out of my office with wetness over his shirt. I was sure that would get us both in trouble.
He laughed at me. "You scared someone will know what it is?"
"Discretion", I replied, rubbing his cheek. He thought for a second.
"Go sit in your chair" he said. I walked over slowly, while he watched me. I sat my wet ass down and watched him walk over to me while he took his tie off and unbuttoned his shirt. The way he did it turned me on even more. He picked one of my legs up and propped it on my desk. Then he spread my other leg the opposite way, making my legs wider for him. He sat his tie on my desk and got on his knees.
"That's a pretty pussy." He said, kissing her. He was so talented with his tongue. He knew exactly how to angle

me to give me the best sensations. I tried my hardest not to moan loudly but every now and then, they escaped my mouth. He sucked my clitoris with his gorgeous lips and soft tongue. That orgasm was creeping in.

"Shit, Alex." I moaned.

He gave a low chuckle, knowing how good his licks were. He rocked my chair back and forth, giving me a ride I'd never forget.

All of a sudden, there was a knock on my office door. We both froze and were quiet for a minute, hoping the person would go away.

I heard another knock, accompanied with "Sonya, its David. You got a minute?"

"SHIT!" I exclaimed. "It's my boss" I told Alex. I stood up to pull my skirt down and realized my panties were still on the floor. I ran over to grab my panties and heard the door crack open. I immediately crumpled them in my hand behind my back.

"Can I come in?" David asked through the crack. Alex scrambled underneath my desk with the quickness. I walked hurriedly over to my chair to sit down.

"Sure." I said, opening one of my drawers to hide my panties in.

David walked in with a huge grin on his face. "Happy Valentine's day, Sonya."

"Happy Valentine's day." I said, still feeling tingles between my legs. I cracked a fake smile and scooted up to my desk, acting as normal as possible.

"When did you start wearing ties?" He asked, referring to Alex's tie on my desk. In my rush, I forgot to hide it.

"Oh, I found it in my purse. It was from an old ummm... boyfriend of mine. I was going to throw it away." I lied.

"Well, that's unfortunate. That's a nice tie." He said, smiling.

"It is. But what's up?" I asked him. I needed him to get to the point so he could get out.

"Oh, nothing, I was just um..." He tried to gather his thoughts. He seemed nervous. As I waited for him to answer, I felt Alex under my desk, trying to pull my skirt back up. I tried to keep my composure. My mind was focused on my boss but my privates were still craving Alex. I scooted to the edge of my chair and felt Alex open my legs under the desk.

"Well, It's Valentine's day and I was just wondering if you had any ideas. Any tips you could give me for my wife. I was trying to do something out of the ordinary."

I felt that soft tongue on my pussy again. It made me stutter. "I-I-umm... Maybe you should try some poetry. There's an event at Berkley's theatre tonight. I was actually going to go... ummm", I stuttered again. Alex was sucking the shit out of my pussy. "I was um... Going to go... ummm." I shook my head, unsure if I could continue this conversation with a straight face.

"You okay?" David asked.

I put my hands to my face "Umm yea, I'm not feeling well. I will email you the information about the event before you leave. Is that okay?" Suddenly, I felt Alex making circles around my clitoris. Putting pressure right under the hood of it when he circled around it. I lost it. "Awww man," I said out loud. I balled my hand into a fist and bit it. "I think I'm going to be sick David, can you leave and shut the door please?" I said, trying to cover my pleasure with a look of pain.

"Okay, but do you need-"

"Nope.... Nope, I'm fine. Thanks. I'll email you" I said, panting. I felt myself about to cum.

"Alright, well let me know if you need something." He said, opening the door. He tried to get one last word in before he left. "And thanks for-"

"Please David, close the door! Give me a minute." I said loudly. He closed the door . I laid back in my seat, grabbing Alex's head and preparing myself for the eruption.

"yessssss..." I moaned, cuming into his tongue. He loved every second of the twitching I did while I came.

"Happy Valentine's Day, Sonya." He said pulling his face up from me, and smiling.

I couldn't believe I got licked while my boss was in my office. We would've been fired on the spot if David would have come around my desk. This was an experience worth getting in trouble for.

I stood up and licked my juices off his lips... Off his chin... Anywhere I saw his face glistening. As I tongued him down, I unzipped his pants and got acquainted with this thickness. I got on my knees, pressed him against the window and sucked him just like he sucked me, using my hand to extend the feeling of my mouth. I twisted my hand around his veins and sucked at the same time, ferociously. The adrenaline from almost getting caught had me beasting on his dick. He sucked in air and let out "Ahhh." sounds. I wanted to taste him. I wasn't typically a swallower, but I wanted to do it for him. He deserved it.

"Cum right here" I whispered to him, sticking my tongue out. I yanked on him and kept my mouth open for his candy. He came on cue, oozing onto my tongue. He was so delicious.

"Happy Valentines Day, Alex." I said to him, sucking on him until he was completely soft again. I yanked his pants back up, tucked him into his boxer briefs, and buckled his pants. I sat on the edge of my desk, taking in what happened. He was still leaning against my window. We were quiet for a while, looking at each other and smiling, trying to figure out what to say. He walked over to me and put his hands on my shoulders. I reached over to grab his tie and tied it back around his neck.

"What time do you get off?" He asked.

"Four thirty." I replied, looking up at him. He put his hands around my face.

"Have dinner with me tonight?"

"Absolutely." I said, completely lost in his stare. "What time?"

"Seven." He took a thin sharpie from beside me, pulled my shirt down, wrote his number on my breast, and then kissed between them. "I'll pick you up." He said, before he touched those beautiful lips to mine. He obviously had future plans for us. And while dating a fellow supervisor was probably not a popular choice, I was willing to give it a try. When he left my office, I giggled to myself. Orgasms are one hell of a gift. That accidental comment brought me one of the best Valentine's Day experiences I had had in a long time... And it all started with a kiss from his lips that I'd never forget...

Starbucks

Dear 6'1, 22 year old Starbucks employee...
You gon' stop looking at me like that.
Like when I come in at 6:45 every morning,
You aren't wanting to be reason I'm always so sleepy.
The way you say "Yes Ma'am" with that smirk on your face,
Has me looking at you like I looked at Chris Brown when "Poppin" came out,
so don't think that our age difference
Don't make me jump over this counter and
Make you give me a few pumps of espresso
Where it counts.
My lips are full of caffeine ready to plant kisses
where I know it excites,
And I'm still a Thunder cat purring with curiosity,
With claws so sharp,
Your back will be a scratching post...

You gon' stop grinning at me like
Your thick ass lips weren't created for
Head first mouth dives in the Atlantic.
I can tell that you suck out souls
More than Joel Olsten on a Sunday,
And I'm ready to baptize you...
yes, I know CPR
Because the way drowning in my waters is set up,
It's easy to get that lost in the sauce,
And if you do, it WILL take 3 business days, to fully recover...

And, you gon' stop calling me "beautiful"
Like I'm not an Equestrian,
ready to ride Pony's to the beat better than
Ginuwine to a Timbaland melody,

I've trained even the most inexperienced of Stallions,
to gallop to the rhythm of my backshot.
And I was raised in the south,
so I spent time on farm lands,
learning proper ways to hog tie or handcuff
my breakfast...
I'd Reverse Cowgirl you so thoroughly,
that I could make you a college dropout,
Boy,
You're one shape up away from me helping your beard
grow in.
One "How Can I help you today?" from me helping
myself.
One "Would you like whip cream on that?" away from
Me putting it on you,
And Age ain't nothing but a damn number so,
So hurry up with my Mocha Frappuccino
before I find out what 22 can do.

Rocking Cradles

Spending time with my best friend and her family was always time well spent. Gina's parents were having a get together to celebrate their 24th anniversary. Any excuse to get the family together was an excuse they took advantage of. Because I had been Gina's best friend since we were 6, I was automatically invited to all their events. And as a hopeless romantic, I didn't want to miss an opportunity to celebrate love.

"Child, I didn't love this man! I damn sure didn't want to marry him!" Her mother howled. Gina's mom was telling us a story about how when she got engaged to Gina's father, she wasn't in love with him. "I was in love with the fact that he supported and spoiled me. That's what I loved. He wanted to take care of me and provide. Other than that, he was boring." She said laughing. We laughed with her.

"Am I still boring?" He asked her, with his arm around the back of her chair.

"Of course not sweetie. I changed all of that. It was a fair exchange." She said before she gave him a peck on the cheek. I loved Gina's parents. Mr. and Mrs. Greene seemed to have the most fun in their relationship. Always so open and honest and having good wholesome fun. I dreamt of having a relationship like that. I just wasn't sure if I could marry someone I didn't love.

"Nevia is dating a boring dude too!" Gina said, giving me the side eye. I looked at her with my eyes wide, wondering why she brought me into this conversation.

"That's not true." I said to everyone.

"Well what's his problem, then?" Gina's cousin asked me.

"Hold on, I'm eating" I said, sticking a forkful of food in my mouth. Everybody laughed again. We all had alcohol in our system so we were loud, talking over each other.
"No seriously, he's not boring. He's just really busy a lot. We don't talk a whole bunch and when we do, it seems like he is distracted."
"He's busy huh?" Mrs. Greene asked, drinking her glass of wine. "Sounds like he has his priorities in order, and you aren't one."
"See? That's exactly what I told her!" Gina responded, in agreement.
"But anytime I try to end things, he pleads with me, saying that he really is busy and just wants me to be patient with him."
"Let me tell you something." Mr Greene started, "When I met my wife, I was working 3 jobs and barely had enough time to sleep. But I always made time for her. Even if it meant cutting back a couple hours here and there at work just to take her somewhere, or missing my sleep all together. I made time. Men make time for women when they want them. End it and then tell him he can make another attempt when he has the time. But make sure he knows you are NOT waiting for him!" Mr. Greene was clearly giving my busy boo the benefit of the doubt. While Mrs. Greene just thought he was full of shit all together.
"Anybody want another drink?" Mrs. Greene asked, lifting her glass in the air. It was empty for the 3rd time. Everybody asked for a refill, including me. She left the table to grab the wine and liquor from the kitchen.
"Thanks for spilling my beans before I could spill them" I said to Gina sarcastically.
"Oh girl, nobody is judging you. I just thought it correlated." She said with a chuckle.
"Correlated, my ass. You put me on the spot." I said smirking. I leaned over to take a sip out of my glass but my tongue couldn't find the straw. The alcohol was getting to me.

"You good Nev?" she asked seeing my coordination was leaving me. We both busted out laughing.
"forget it." I said taking the straw out to sip from the glass. Gina got up to get more chips for us. A couple minutes later I heard a knock at the door. "I'll get it!" I yelled, since I was closest to the door.
Without looking through the peep hole, I opened the door, and was stuck.
"Damn." I said looking him up and down.
"Hey Nev. How are you?" He said hugging me. His hug was so firm and his back was strong, I could tell. After we hugged, I leaned away from him, trying to put this puzzle together.
"Wait... Corey?" I asked.
"That would be me." He said smiling. Corey was Gina's younger brother. He was 24 and doing very well as a grad student at Hampton University. I hadn't seen Corey since he was in middle school, when Gina and I were both doing our junior year in college. Corey did a major 180 from the skinny, big-headed troublemaker that I remembered. Shit, I almost thought Gina's mom had hired a fine ass stripper or something for the party. Corey was so damn thick and delicious looking with that light beard on his face. I was in shock.
"COREY!" Gina yelled, running past me into his arms. Ashamed of my dirty thoughts for my best friends little brother, I turned around to go sit back down at the table and sip my refilled glass of wine. When he made it to the kitchen, Mrs. Greene showered her son with kisses. Corey had always been a mommas boy, even when we were younger. I guess that never changed.
"How long was your drive, son?" Mr. Greene asked.
"Five hours." Corey said taking a seat across from me.
"Well that's not bad. Must not have been any traffic."
"Not at all. The roads were surprisingly traffic free today."
"where's your little girlfriend?" Gina asked jokingly.
"My what?" Corey asked rhetorically.
"Oh, so ya'll broke up?"

"That's a long story that I don't want to get into." He said chuckling.
"Well you can tell me later. For now, let's eat! I'm hungry!" Gina said jumping up to get her food.
Finally it was dinner time. We all filled our plate with delicious food Mr. Greene had catered from a local soul food spot. When I tell you the beef ribs were hittin'! They had all of us licking our fingers at that dinner table. By that time everybody was damn near drunk. I just drank to maintain my tipsiness.
"You sure you don't want a drink, Corey?" Mr. Greene asked his son.
"No Dad, I'm fine. I have some school work I need to finish back at the hotel.
"Why did you get a hotel anyway? You could've stayed here." Mrs. Greene asked.
"And Listen to ya'll attempt to have sex? Nah, I'm good." Corey said. We all laughed.
"Attempt? Boy, this grown folk love making over here! I still gets it done! Believe me!"
"Ewww!" Gina said, frowning.
"Alright, that's enough" Corey said throwing his hands up. "I don't want to hear about it."
"You okay over there, Nev? You haven't hardly spoken since we got our food." Mrs. Greene asked me. I couldn't tell her the reason for my silence was because I was undressing her son in my mind at the dinner table.
"Oh yea. I'm fine. This food is just really really good."
"Yea it is." Corey said. "Where have you been anyway, Nev? I feel like I haven't seen you in forever."
"Well, you know I was in Cali for a while, being a wife." I said sipping from my glass.
"Yea, I heard about that. I'm sorry it didn't work out."
"Oh, its fine. It couldn't have happened any other way. I'm just glad we don't have any kids together to worry about."
"Be thankful for that." Mrs. Greene added.
"Yea." Gina interjected, "Now she's moved on to better and more boring men."

I cut my eyes at her. "Really, Gina?" Everybody at the table laughed. "You know what, that's my cue." I said getting up from the table.
"Oh, come on, I was just kidding." Gina said.
"I know, girl. But I really am starting to get sleepy. This food is giving me the itis. I need to go ahead on home." ... *and try not to think about fucking your brother...* I thought.
"Oh alright," Mrs. Greene said. "Well you take a plate with you. You know we hate leftovers."
"Sure thing." I said making my plate to go. On my way to retrieve my purse, I tripped and almost fell. I was still intoxicated.
"You okay?" Mr. Greene asked me.
"Yea I'm fine." I said trying to compose myself.
"Wait a minute, let somebody drive you home. You've been drinking all night."
"No, I'm not far, I can make it." I said, unsure if I actually was going to be able to make it.
"No, let me drive you home." Corey suggested.
"Yea, let Corey do it. He's the only non-drunk person in here."
"But my car..."
"it's the weekend. I can pick you back up in the morning to get it." He said, nonchalantly. I would've let anybody else drive me home but Corey. I was lusting on him too hard for this. But everybody else was intoxicated as well. I didn't have a choice.
"Fine."
"Good. Let me grab your plate for you." He said, coming over to take the plate. I went around the table to hug everyone before Corey and I walked out the house. He went to the passenger side to open my door first.
"Such a gentleman." I said.
"My dad would kill me If I wasn't." He said smiling. He put my plate in the back seat and hopped in the car to begin the drive.
"So where do you live now?" he asked me.
"Near Crosswalk drive. Near the new shopping center."

"Okay, I know where that is. That's real convenient. The Harris Teeter over this is nice too. I bet the neighborhood is nice."
"Oh yea. Mixed area. Quiet. Just how I like it."
"Yea, I like mixed places too. Even though I go to Hampton U, I do NOT live hear the college."
"You don't like black people either sometimes, huh?" I said laughing and settling into my seat.
"I love my people. I just hate their shenanigans. When it's great, we have a great time. When it's bad, it gets completely out of hand. When I joined my frat, I got a load of it for the first couple years. Fights for nothing, ridiculous stuff with women..."
"What? You joined a fraternity? Which one?" He smirked and made a sign with his hand. "Oh shit..." I said, recognizing that sign and remembering my college days. I got in some serious trouble messing with a couple guys in that fraternity. My ex-husband was in it too. Trouble in all aspects.
"What you say that for? You don't like my frat?" He said jokingly.
"Listen, they ran my campus. Any drama happening on campus was always somehow linked to them!" I said laughing. "But if they caused trouble at your school, then I guess nothing has changed over the years. And that was a looonnnngggg time ago."
"You say that like you're 50." He said looking over at me.
"Because I am." I said. We laughed.
"Seriously, how old are you now? 27?"
I cut my eyes at him "Real cute, Corey." I wasn't sure if he was being sweet or outright flirting with me.
"But really, you look 27 at the most." He was definitely flirting.
"A genuine compliment. Thank you." I said.
"No problem. I give them where they are due."
"And you're over there looking like a grown ass man." I was secretly looking at his body while he drove. He smiled.
"I am a grown ass man." He reminded me.

"You're right Corey. You just started grad school and you are handling your business. You're doing better than many of the dudes my age."
"Yea, that's because many of the dudes your age are chasing women MY age. They aren't ready to settle."
"That's very true. I thought the older I got, the less games they'd play. But these guys out here aren't done playing games. They just have gotten better at the games they are playing." There was a moment of silence.
"So would you be opposed to dating a younger guy?" he asked me.
"How much younger are we talking?"
"I don't know, my age. 9 years younger." We looked at each other for a moment before I laughed. "What's so funny?"
"Nine years? Sheesh, Corey. When I was in college you were still in middle school. I'd feel like I was dating a baby. I'd be a cougar." I was so conflicted. Younger men just weren't my thing... except Corey. He was just too damn fine. He was the ONLY exception.
"You'd be a fine Cougar though. With a young man on your arm. All your friends would be jealous, right?" He said smirking.
"Oh stop it." I said loving his compliments.
He began imitating the voices of women. "Ohh Girl, did you see Nevia with that fine ass man? She think she's hot stuff now. I bet he won't stay with her. I bet he will cheat!" I was cracking up.
"Why would a young guy want me anyway? He should be out here sowing his seeds with these young girls."
"Not all of us are assholes trying to get a nut, Nev. Some of us have standards."
"So you weren't in college whoring around? Is that what you are saying?" He paused. "Yea that's what I thought."
He laughed, "Listen, I've done some dirt, broken some hearts and had some sexual conquests like any other man. But I've learned from all that. I personally just want one woman to put all my seeds into. In her womb or in her mouth, either is cool."

"Ewww Corey!" I said laughing. He smiled.
"Is this your street right here?" He asked. We were coming up on my house.
"Yea, at the end of this street, make a right and it's the 4th house on the right." I hated the car ride was over.
He pulled up to my house in my parking lot. I wasn't ready to leave. "So you going back to the hotel after you leave here or are you going back to your parent's?"
"I'm going to the hotel. I really do have to finish this work for school before I head back Sunday. And I'm really not trying to hear my parents do whatever kind of celebrations they are going to do." I grinned.
"I guess you're never too old." I said.
"Never." He said before he got out of the car. He came to my side to open my door for me. Forcing me to leave the car. I wanted him to take me back to the hotel with him. Or Stay at my place. But I didn't want to disrupt his school work. He followed me to my porch.
"Thank you." I said to him. We were standing right in front of my front door.
"No problem. Oh, I forgot to give you my number so you could call me in the morning to get your car."
"Oh yea." I said, pulling my phone out to save his number. He gave me his digits and I saved it and called him to make sure he had mine. Then we stood there, waiting for something to happen. It was dark and warm outside. My body was dark and my temperature was heating up with anxiousness. "Are you going to go inside?" He asked, with his hands in his pockets.
"Yea, in a minute." I said, stalling. I put my back against the door and dropped my purse. He went to pick it up.
"No." I said, stopping him. "Leave it." He stood back up slowly staring at me the whole time. The sexual tension was strong. I knew that he knew what I wanted. But I wanted him to take it. I didn't want to make the first move. He put his arms on the door on both sides of me, and leaned into me.
"Is there something you want?" He asked.
"Maybe."

"Maybe? Well if you don't want it that bad then maybe you shouldn't have-"

"-Yes" I said, interrupting him and changing my answer.

"And what is it that you want?" He pushed up against me. I put my hands behind my back, trying not to touch him. He rubbed his face against mine as if he was about to lick my ear, but he didn't. I could feel his breath right under my earlobe. That made the tiny hairs all over me stand up, giving me chills. He ran his lips across my face, but didn't kiss me. I wanted him to kiss me, but he kept trying to force me to make the first move.

"Tell me what you want, Nev." He whispered to me, his mouth barely touching my ear. He was pulling the cougar out of me. My animalistic impulses were surfacing. I placed a kiss on his neck. Then another. Then I stuck my tongue out to taste his skin.

"Mmmm." He said. I pulled away from him to look in his face. I wanted him to grab me, pick me up, kick my door down and fuck me like the gorilla linked to his fraternity. But he didn't. He wanted me to do more.

"You aren't telling me what you want, Nev." He said. I tugged on his shirt, and let my forehead rest on his chin. This was killing me. "I should leave." He said, pulling away from me as if he was about to go back to his car. I grasped his shirt tighter, and forcefully pulled him back to me. Then I put my hands up his shirt and felt his chest, running my nails down the ridges in his abs. I leaned in to kiss him hard. He put his wet thick tongue in my mouth, giving my lips the gratification they wanted. I put my arms around his waist and slid my hands in his pants in the back, grabbing his ass and pushing his pelvis toward mine. I wanted to feel his dick. His sweat pants made it easy to feel.

"I want you to fuck me." I whispered.

"I can do that..." He said, unzipping my pants and pulling them down to my ankles. We did all of this right on the porch in front of my house. My neighborhood was quiet and I couldn't imagine anybody being out this late, but unless they were the police, I didn't care.

Corey pulled pants down in the front enough for his sack and dick to come out. He pushed me against my door and rubbed that long snake between my pussy lips. He managed to get it inside of me, chest to chest, with my pants around my ankles. The passion was intense. The way we were positioned had his dick rubbing like shit against my clitoris while he slid in and out. It felt so good.

"Uhhhh" I moaned...

"Shhhhhh..." He said, not wanting to disturb any neighbors. I bit his shoulder through his shirt. The cougar was definitely out of her cage. I dug my nails into his back. I wanted to feel him deeper so I managed to get one leg out of my jeans, and wrapped it around him. He pulled me close and breathed heavily in my ear. Doing this in public and trying to stay quiet, was adding on to my arousal. Each stroke hit my clitoris like a massage. Like he the veins in his dick were kneading it. I held Corey by his waist, feeling myself about to cum.

"Coreeeyyyy." I called out, mouth wide open.

"Shhhh... shhhhh..." He said to me again. When I couldn't get my groans under control, he began kissing me, trying to muffle my sounds. The sounds of our torsos hitting each other was just as loud, if not louder. He grabbed my ass cheeks, and squeezed them as I came. My breath was trembling. He slowed his pace and pulled out, with his dick and my thighs glossy from my wetness. He looked at me while I panted and tried to regain some energy to lift my back off of my door.

"Why didn't you finish?" I asked him.

"I did. What do you mean?"

"You didn't cum."

He grinned at me. "I don't always have to cum." He said. "Feeling you cum was satisfying enough."

I was completely wrong about my assumption about "Younger" guys. I was sure Corey was going to cum fast and leave me high and dry. He did exactly what I asked him to do. Fucked me.

I pulled my pants up and he put his snake back in his sweat pants. It was still hard and swinging since he refused to cum.
"Anymore orders before I go?" he asked, smirking. I smirked back.
"You know we can't tell anybody about this. Your sister would kill me."
"I know how to keep secrets, Nev. I'm not 10 anymore."
"You're right." I said, tugging at his shirt to signal him to kiss him again. A couple hours ago I couldn't even look Corey in his face. Now, I couldn't keep myself off of him. "You can't stay?"
"I have school work to do, remember?"
"Oh yea." I said. I completely forgot about that. "You can't do it here?"
"My books are back at the hotel."
I sighed. He shook his head. "This was only a one-time thing, right?"
"Of course." I said, with a fake smile. Something about that young energy was giving me energy and I needed more. I turned to open my door, stepped in and turned back around. "One more time...." I said seductively.
He shook his head, grinning. "You don't want me to get anything done do you?"
"Of course I do.... I'd like it if you got me done..."
He paused. "One more time?"
"Maybe two more."
"Nev..."
"Corey..."
I could see him struggling. He was a disciplined student. But an even more disciplined lover. I pulled him into my house by his sweatpants... Fuck school work. I just wanted him to work me....

www.ingramcontent.com/pod-product-compliance
Lightning Source LLC
LaVergne TN
LVHW020655100826
845148LV00012B/2507
* 9 7 8 1 7 3 3 0 5 0 2 5 8 *